Augusta
of Hesse-Cassel
1797 – 1889

Adolphus,
Duke of Cambridge
1774 – 1850

Countess Claudine
Rhéday, Countess
of Hohenstein
1812 – 1841

Mary Adelaide
of Cambridge
1833 – 1897

Mary of Teck
1867 – 1953

Francis, Duke of Teck
1837 – 1900

Duke Alexander
of Württemberg
1804 – 1885

King George VI
1895 – 1952

Qu
Eliza
f 1
192

King George V
1865 – 1936

Louise of
Hesse-Cassel
1817 – 1898

Alexandra of Denmark
1844 – 1925

King Edward VII
1841 – 1910

Christian IX
King of Denmark
1818 – 1906

Prince Albert
of Saxe-Coburg
and Gotha
1819 – 1861

Queen Victoria
1819 – 1901

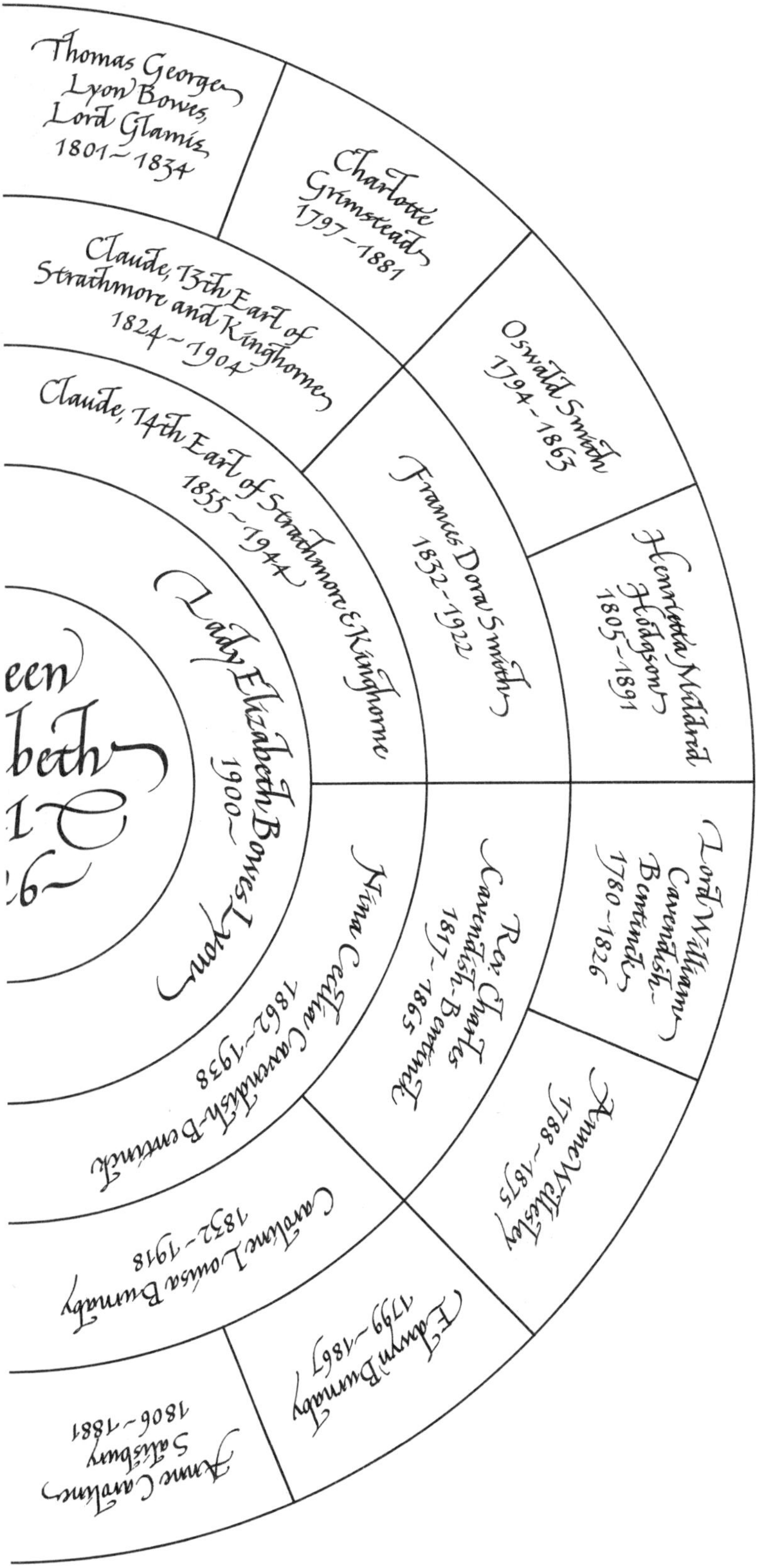

Thomas George Lyon Bowes, Lord Glamis, 1801~1834
Charlotte Grimstead 1797~1881
Claude, 13th Earl of Strathmore and Kinghorne 1824~1904
Oswald Smith 1794~1863
Claude, 14th Earl of Strathmore & Kinghorne 1855~1944
Frances Dora Smith 1832~1922
Henrietta Mildred Hodgson 1805~1891
een
beth
1
6
Lady Elizabeth Bowes Lyon 1900~
Lord William Cavendish Bentinck 1780~1826
Rev. Charles Cavendish-Bentinck 1817~1865
Nina Cecilia Cavendish-Bentinck 1862~1938
Anne Wellesley 1788~1875
Caroline Louisa Burnaby 1832~1918
Edwyn Burnaby 1799~1867
Anne Caroline Salisbury 1806~1881

THE QUEEN

THE QUEEN

A Biography of Elizabeth II

BEN PIMLOTT

John Wiley & Sons, Inc.

New York • Chichester • Weinheim • Brisbane • Singapore • Toronto

Copyright © 1996 by Ben Pimlott
First published in the United States by John Wiley & Sons, Inc., 1997
All rights reserved. Published simultaneously in Canada.

First published in Great Britain in 1996 by HarperCollins*Publishers*.

Calligraphy by David Williams

Library of Congress Cataloging-in-Publication Data

Pimlott, Ben.
    The Queen : a biography of Elizabeth II / Ben Pimlott.
      p. cm.
    Originally published: London : HarperCollins, 1996.
    Includes bibliographical references and index.
    ISBN 0-471-19431-X (cloth : alk. paper)
    1. Elizabeth II, Queen of Great Britain, 1926–   . 2. Great
Britain—History—Elizabeth II, 1952–   3. Queens—Great Britain—
Biography. I. Title.
DA590.P54 1997
941.085′092—dc21
[B]   97-21270

Printed in the United States of America

10 9 8 7 6 5 4 3 2 1

To my family

LIST OF PLATES

Prince Philip and Princess Elizabeth at the wedding of Lord Brabourne and Patricia Mountbatten at Romsey, 1946 (*Topham*)

Princess Elizabeth during a deck game on HMS *Vanguard*, April 1947 (*Popperfoto*)

Princess Elizabeth and Princess Margaret riding on the seashore in South Africa, 1947 (*The Royal Archives © 1996 Her Majesty Queen Elizabeth II*)

Between pages 268–269

Princess Elizabeth and Prince Philip on their wedding day, November 1947 (*Hulton Getty Picture Collection*)

Princess Elizabeth arriving at Westminster Abbey with her father for her marriage to Prince Philip, November 1947 (*Hulton Getty Picture Collection*)

Prince Charles with Princess Elizabeth and Prince Philip, July 1949 (*Hulton Getty Picture Collection*)

Princess Elizabeth and the Queen at Hurst Park Races, January 1952 (*Hulton Getty Picture Collection*)

Princess Elizabeth with Mountbatten at a ball at the Savoy, 3rd July 1951 (*Hulton Getty Picture Collection*)

The Queen arriving at Clarence House after her father's death, 7th February 1952 (*Hulton Getty Picture Collection*)

The Queen as she drives to Westminster for the State Opening of Parliament, 1952 (*Hulton Getty Picture Collection*)

The Coronation of Queen Elizabeth II showing the Queen wearing her crown and preparing to receive homage, 2nd June 1953 (*Hulton Getty Picture Collection*)

The Queen Mother with Prince Charles at the Coronation, 2nd June 1953 (*Hulton Getty Picture Collection*)

Queen Elizabeth holding a model zebra with Princess Elizabeth, Peter Townsend and Princess Margaret in South Africa, 1947 (*Popperfoto*)

The Queen, and the Duke of Edinburgh with Sir Anthony and Lady Eden, 25th July 1955 (*Popperfoto*)

Daily Mirror front page 'Smack! Lord A. gets his face slapped,' 7th August 1957 (*By permission of the British Library/Mirror Syndication International*)

Sir Michael Adeane (*Godfrey Argent for the Archives of the National Portrait Gallery/Camera Press London*)

The Queen with various members of the Government including Harold Macmillan, 16th February 1957 (*Hulton Getty Picture Collection*)

The Queen with Charles de Gaulle at Covent Garden, April 1960 (*Hulton Getty Picture Collection*)

The Queen with her corgis, 8th February 1968 (*Hulton Getty Picture Collection*)

Between pages 428–429

The Queen on *Britannia*, 1972 (*Patrick Lichfield/Camera Press London*)

The Queen with Princess Anne, 1965 (*Camera Press London*)

The Investiture of the Prince of Wales, 1st July 1969 (*Hulton Getty Picture Collection*)

The Queen with Lord Porchester, 1966 (*Hulton Getty Picture Collection*)

The Queen at Aberfan, 29th October 1966 (*Hulton Getty Picture Collection*)

A student drinks from a bottle in front of the Queen at Stirling University, 12th October 1972 (© Scotsman Publications)

The Queen with Sir Martin Charteris on board *Britannia*, 31st October 1972 (*Patrick Lichfield/Camera Press London*)

The Queen on a Jubilee walkabout, 20th June 1977 (*Ian Berry/Magnum Photos*)

The Queen, Prince Philip and Prince Charles in Australia, 1970: 'as short as we dared' (*by permission of Sir Hardy Amies*)

The Queen with Harold Wilson, 24th March 1976 (*Hulton Getty Picture Collection*)

Prince Andrew returns from the Falklands, 1982 (*Bryn Colton/Camera Press London*)

The Queen with Margaret Thatcher and Hastings Banda, 3rd August 1979 (*Hulton Getty Picture Collection*)

Princess Elizabeth with President Truman, 4th November 1951 (*Hulton Getty Picture Collection*)

The Queen with Prince Philip and the Kennedys, 6th June 1961 (*Hulton Getty Picture Collection*)

The Queen with President Carter and Prince Philip, 10th May 1977 (*Hulton Getty Picture Collection*)

The Queen riding with President Reagan in Windsor Great Park, 1982 (*Tim Graham*)

The Queen and Prince Philip with the Clintons, 29th November 1995 (*Tim Graham*)

The Queen with a fireman at Windsor Castle, 21st November 1992 (*Hulton Getty Picture Collection/Reuters*)

The Queen watches Jürgen Klinsmann holding the European championship trophy, 30th June 1996 (*Marc Aspland/Times Newspapers*)

CARTOONS

PREFACE

'What a marvellous way of looking at the history of Britain', said Raphael Samuel, when I told him about this book. Some others expressed surprise, wondering whether a study of the Head of State and Head of the Commonwealth could be a serious or worthwhile enterprise. Whether or not they are right, it has certainly been an extraordinary and fascinating adventure: partly because of the fresh perspective on familiar events it has given me, after years of writing about Labour politicians; partly because of the human drama of a life so exceptionally privileged, and so exceptionally constrained; and partly because of the obsession with royalty of the British public, of which I am a member. Perhaps the last has interested me most of all. To some extent, therefore, this is a book about the Queen in people's heads, as well as at Buckingham Palace. It is, of course, incomplete – no work could be more 'interim' than an account of a monarch who may still have decades to reign. However, because the story is still going on with critical chapters yet to come, it is also – more than most biographies – concerned with now.

It is an 'unofficial' study, and draws eclectically on a variety of sources. For the period up to 1952, the Royal Archives have been invaluable; documentation up to the mid or late 1960s has been provided by the Public Record Office and the BBC Written Archive Centre, alongside a number of private collections of papers, listed at the end of this book. For later years, interviews have been particularly helpful. In addition, there is a wealth of published material.

I have a great many individual debts. I am extremely grateful to Sir Robert Fellowes (Private Secretary to the Queen and Keeper of the Royal Archives), Charles Anson (Press Secretary to the Queen), Oliver Everett (Assistant Keeper of the Royal Archives) and Sheila de Bellaigue (Registrar of the Royal Archives) for assisting with my requests whenever it was possible to do so.

I would like to thank Anne Pimlott Baker, principal researcher for the book, for the care and resourcefulness of her inquiries, and for her skilful digests and research notes; Andrew Chadwick, for research into the archives of *The Times* and *News of the World*; Sarah Benton, for reading the whole text in draft and making many perceptive comments on it; Anne-Marie Rule for typing the manuscript with her usual combination of speed, precision and good-natured tolerance of unreasonable demands – the fifth time she has typed a book for me (am I the last author, incidentally, who still uses a pen and has his drafts typed on a pre-electric typewriter?); Terry Mayer and Jane Tinkler for their help in typing, and retyping, some of the chapters, and for many kindnesses; and my colleagues and students at Birkbeck, for their forebearance, interest and encouragement.

I am grateful to the many librarians and archivists, in the United Kingdom and elsewhere, who have helped me in person, on the telephone, or by correspondence. In addition to those already mentioned, I would especially like to thank Jacquie Kavanagh at the BBC Written Archive Centre at Caversham Park, Helen Langley at the Bodleian Library and the library staff of The Times Newspapers and the *Guardian*. I am also particularly grateful to Sir Hardy Amies, for generously making available to me his coresspondence with the Queen and members of the Royal Family over a period of more than forty years; to Phillip Whitehead, for letting me see the unedited transcripts of interviews for his television documentary, *The Windsors*; and Vernon Bogdanor and Frank Prochaska for showing me the text of their excellent recent books, before publication. I am deeply indebted to the staff of the British Library at Bloomsbury, who continue to provide an outstanding service, despite trying conditions during the countdown to the move (regretted by so many) to St Pancras.

I am grateful to the following for permission to quote copyright material: Arrow Books (D. Morrah *To Be a King*); Collins (H. Nicolson *Diaries and Letters 1930–1939*); Duckworth (M. Crawford *The Little Princesses*); Hamish Hamilton (R. Crossman *The Backbench Diaries of Richard Crossman*; *The Diaries of a Cabinet Minister 1964–66*); Hutchinson (T. Benn *Out of the Wilderness: Diaries 1963–67*); Macmillan (J. Wheeler-Bennett *George VI: His Life and Reign*).

I would like to acknowledge the gracious permission of Her Majesty the Queen for allowing me the privilege of using the Royal Archives at Windsor Castle, and for granting me permission to quote from papers in the Archives. For the use of other unpublished papers and documents I am grateful to: Sir Hardy Amies (Amies papers); Lady Avon (Avon papers); Balliol College, Oxford (Nicolson papers); BBC Written Archive Centre (BBC Written Archives); British Library of Political and Economic Science (Dalton papers); Christ Church, Oxford (Bradwell papers); Churchill College, Cambridge (Alexander papers; Chartwell papers; Swinton papers); Lady Margaret Colville (Colville papers); Dwight D. Eisenhower Library (Eisenhower papers); Mrs Caroline Erskine (Lascelles papers); House of Lords (Beaverbrook papers); John F. Kennedy Library (Kennedy papers); Lambeth

Palace (Fisher papers); F. D. Roosevelt Library (Roosevelt papers); Harry S. Truman Library (Truman papers); University College, Oxford (Attlee papers); University of Southampton (Mountbatten papers).

I would like to thank the following people who have taken the time to talk to me about different aspects of this book: Lord Airlie, Lady Airlie, Ronald Allison, Sir Hardy Amies, Lord Armstrong of Ilminster, Sir Shane Blewitt, Lord Brabourne, Sir Alistair Burnet, Lord Buxton, Lord Callaghan, Lord Carnarvon, Lady Carnarvon, Lord Carrington, Lady Elizabeth Cavendish, Lord Charteris, Lord Cranborne, Jonathan Dimbleby, Lord Egremont, Sir Edward Ford, Princess George of Hanover, The Duchess of Grafton, John Grigg, Joe Haines, David Hicks, Lady Pamela Hicks, Anthony Holden, Angela Howard-Johnston, Lord Howe, Lord Hunt of Tamworth, Douglas Hurd, Sir Bernard Ingham, Michael Jones, Robin Janvrin, Lord Limerick, Lady Longford, Brian MacArthur, Lord McNally, HRH Princess Margaret, Sir John Miller, Sir Derek Mitchell, Lady Mountbatten, Michael Noakes, The Duke of Norfolk, Commander Michael Parker, Michael Peat, Rt Rev Simon Phipps, Sir Edward Pickering, Sir David Pitblado, Sir Charles Powell, Enoch Powell, Sir Sonny Ramphal, Sir John Riddell, Kenneth Rose, Lord Runcie, Sir Kenneth Scott, Michael Shea, Phillip Whitehead, Sir Clive Whitmore and Mrs Woodroffe. I also spoke to others who prefer not to be named. Where it has not been possible to give the source of a quotation in the text or notes, I have used the words 'Confidential interview'. None of these people, or anybody else apart from the author, is responsible for how the material has been interpreted.

HarperCollins has once again proved itself the Rolls Royce of British non-fiction publishing. I am particularly indebted to Stuart Proffitt, my publisher, for his persistent faith in the project and his shrewd author management, and to my incomparable editor, Arabella Quin, for whom my admiration has no bounds. I am also grateful to Caroline Wood for her inspired picture research, and to Anne O'Brien for vital last-minute help. Giles Gordon, my literary agent, has been a constant source of practical wisdom and advice.

Finally, I thank the people to whom the book is dedicated: my children, for keeping my spirits up; and my wife, Jean Seaton, for whom all my books are really written, whose thoughts about monarchy and royalty are now inextricably bound up with my own, and whose fertile historical imagination has been a daily quarry.

Bloomsbury, WC1
August 1996

1

A PRIL 1926 was a busy month for every member of the Conservative Government, but for few ministers more than the Home Secretary, Sir William Joynson-Hicks. A long, bitter dispute in the coalfields was moving rapidly towards its climax – with drastic implications for the nation.

'We are going to be slaves no longer and our men will starve before they accept any reductions in wages,' the miners' leader, A. J. Cook, had declared in an angry speech that crystallized the mood in the collieries, while the men resolved: 'Not a penny off the pay, not a minute on the day'. On 14 April, the TUC leadership asked the Prime Minister to intervene. A week later the owners and men met, but failed to reach agreement. Thereafter, the chance of a compromise diminished, and the prospect grew closer of a terrifying industrial shutdown which – for the first time in British history – seemed likely to affect the majority of British manual workers. Alarm affected all levels of society. Even King George V – mindful of his right to be consulted, and his duty both to encourage and above all to warn – discreetly urged his ministers to show caution. Alas, royal counsels were in vain, and the General Strike began at midnight on 3rd May 1926, threatening not just economic paralysis and bankruptcy, but the constitution itself.

'Jix' Joynson-Hicks – best known to history for his zeal in ordering police raids on the decadent writings of D.H. Lawrence and Radclyffe Hall, and for the part he later played in defeating the 1927 Bill to revise the Prayer Book – was scarcely an outstanding or memorable holder of his post. This, however, was his most splendid hour. In swashbuckling alliance with Winston Churchill, Neville Chamberlain, Quintin Hogg and Leo Amery, the Home Secretary was a Cabinet hawk, in the thick of the fight, a scourge of the miners, opposed to an easy settlement.

If nothing else – it was said – he had nerve. It was Jix who, just after the Strike began, appealed for 50,000 volunteers for the special constables, in order to protect essential vehicles – and thereby raised the temperature of the dispute. For several critical weeks, Jix was at the heart of the nation's events, in constant touch with the Metropolitan Police, and sometimes with the Prime Minister as well.

Sleep was at a premium, snatched between night-time Downing Street parleys and daytime consultations with officials. A call in the early hours of 21 April to attend a royal birth, shortly before one of the most critical meetings in the entire dispute between the Prime Minister and the coal owners, was therefore not entirely a cause for celebration. But it was a duty not to be shirked, and Joynson-Hicks was equal to it. He hurried to the bedside of the twenty-five-year-old Duchess of York, wife of the King's second son, at 17 Bruton Street – the London home of the Duchess's parents, the Earl and Countess of Strathmore, who happened to be among the most prominent coal owners in the United Kingdom. The child was born at 2.40 a.m., and named Elizabeth Alexandra Mary, after the Duchess and two Queens.

Why the Home Secretary needed to attend the birth of the child of a minor member of the Royal Family was one of the mysteries of the British Monarchy. Later, when Princess Elizabeth herself became pregnant, an inquiry was launched at the instigation of the then Labour Home Secretary, Chuter Ede. Inspecting the archives, Home Office researchers rejected as myth a quaint belief, fondly held by the Royal Household and the public alike, that it had something to do with verification, James II and warming pans. After taking expert advice, Ede informed Sir Alan Lascelles, Private Secretary to George VI, that it was no more than 'the custom of past ages by which ministers thronged the private apartments of royalty daily, and particularly at moments of special significance such as births, marriages and deaths'.[1] In 1926, however, it was enough that it was customary – Jix was not the kind of man to question it. According to *The Times* the next day, Sir William 'was present in the house at the time of the birth' and conveyed the news by special messenger to the Lord Mayor.

It was a difficult delivery, despite the best attention. Not until 10 a.m. did the Duchess's doctors issue a guarded statement which revealed what had happened. 'Previous to the confinement a consultation took place,' it declared, '. . . and a certain line of treatment' – decorous code for a Caesarean section – 'was successfully adopted'.[2] The announcement had more than a purely medical significance. The risks such an operation then entailed, and would again entail in the event of subsequent pregnancies, made it unlikely that the Duchess would have a large family, and hence reduced the chances of a future male heir.

At the time, however, few regarded the Princess's proximity to the throne as important. Some later writers, looking back, argued that her succession was always likely.[3] But this was *post hoc*: in 1926 the Duke of York's elder brother was young and healthy, and was expected to marry and have issue. When Princess Elizabeth was born she was third in line for the throne after her uncle, the Prince of Wales, and her father, and under the 1701 Act of Settlement she took precedence over her father's young brothers – just as Queen Victoria had taken precedence over the Duke of Cumberland, younger brother of William IV, in 1837, even though her own father, the Duke of Kent, had predeceased him. Therefore, until either her uncle had a legitimate heir, or her father had a son, Elizabeth's eventual succession was possible, and she had a special standing as a result. But this chance initially seemed remote, and the Princess was much less afflicted during her earliest years by the isolating sense of an inescapable destiny than either her eldest uncle, or her own eldest son.

Despite the distance of the child from the throne, the newspapers took a keen interest in the birth. Perhaps they were responding to the deepening crisis with a bromide, or perhaps it was part of a patriotic reaction. Whatever the cause, far more attention was paid to Princess Elizabeth in 1926 than to George V's first two grandsons, George and Gerald Lascelles, sons of the Princess Royal, in 1923 and 1924, even though at the time of their births they had been similarly placed in the line of succession. Such, indeed, was the excitement that a crowd swiftly gathered in Bruton Street in the hope of seeing the Princess, to greet the messenger boys who arrived with telegrams and presents, and to cheer the Duchess's royal callers.

Among the first to arrive were the King and Queen. 'Such a relief and joy,' wrote Queen Mary in her diary, noting that the baby was 'a little darling with lovely complexion & pretty fair hair'. The Duke of York was beside himself. 'We always wanted a child to make our happiness complete,' he wrote to his mother. Kings, however, prefer male descendants. The Duke therefore added a little anxiously, 'I do hope that you & Papa are as delighted as we are, to have a granddaughter, or would you sooner have another grandson. I know Elizabeth wanted a daughter.'[4]

Then the nation was plunged into turmoil and uncertainty as, for six bewildering days, industries and services were halted, and workers took to the streets. The Duke of York attended debates daily at the House of Commons; at Buckingham Palace, sentries exchanged their red coats for khaki; and the royal entourage was cut to a minimum as an emergency measure, to allow the lords-in-waiting and most of the equerries to take up duties in Jix's army of special constables. Yet public interest in the royal baby was unabated. On 14 May, just after the ending of the Strike, Queen Mary's lady-in-waiting and friend, the Countess of Airlie, visited 17 Bruton Street to deliver the gift of a bottle of 'Jordan water' from the Holy Land, for use at the christening. She found such a throng in the street that the infant had to be taken out for her morning airing by a back entrance.

The christening took place at Buckingham Palace at the end of May, attended by ten 'children of the Chapel Royal' – small boys clad in crimson and gold, with neck jabots of old lace. The Princess wore a skirt several feet in length. She cried so much during the service that immediately after it her old-fashioned nurse surprised 'the modern young mothers present' (as Lady Airlie described some of the Duchess's friends), and much amused the Prince of Wales, by dosing her heavily from a bottle of dill water.[5] In spite of the puckering of the royal features, great interest was shown in the infant's physical appearance. One resourceful sketch-writer wrote of the Princess's 'pure cream complexion and blue eyes fringed with long, dark lashes'.[6]

The baby was no sooner baptized than an active debate began in the press about how she should, and would, be brought up. The issue of modernity versus tradition became a matter of particular concern, especially to women writers in the popular magazines, where prejudice and preference tended to merge with the little evidence that was available about what actually went on. There was also the question of whether royal child-rearing should be special – given the future responsibilities of a member of the Royal Family – or follow a pattern which any mother should treat as the ideal. Most commentators opted for the latter. 'Sensible' was a much favoured word: a sensible nursery regime involved strict, no-nonsense orderliness, with an emphasis on routine, and the avoidance of fads.

Above all – a point on which all agreed – there must be no excessive luxury. A distinction was made between the opulent symbols of royal status, which were considered both acceptable and desirable; and any kind of physical or especially dietary indulgence. Thus, the National Jewellers' Association was applauded for presenting the Princess with a silver porringer, with ivory handles carved in the form of thistles and a cover surmounted by an ivory and silver coronet. There were no objections when the chairman of the Association, Mr G. L. Joseph, declared after a little ceremony at Bruton Street his hope that the porringer would take its place 'upon the breakfast table of the first baby in the land, and may even be banged upon the table by her infant hands'.[7] It was also felt appropriate that royal baby clothes should be hand-made from the finest materials; and there was wide approval at the news that the Queen of England herself, together with Lady Strathmore and the Duchess of York, had personally stitched the Princess's layette, assisted by the inmates of charitable institutions where relevant skills were to be found. 'Many poor gentlewomen,' it was reported, 'have profited by the Duchess's order for fine lawn and muslin frocks, little bonnets and jackets, and all the delightful accessories of baby's toilet.' However, it was simultaneously claimed that, as 'a great believer in modern methods of bringing up infants,' the Duchess of York rejected the arguments of those who favoured long skirts for ordinary use.

Long skirts meant unnecessary waste. Yet if the Duchess was modern on the subject of skirts, she was old-fashioned on the matter of cloth. A battle raged in the 1920s between mothers and nurses who held to the tradition of clothing babies in cotton garments, and progressive advocates of warm, soft, cosy and absorptive wool.[8] The Duchess firmly rejected wool. After visiting a welfare centre where 'woolly babies' were the rule, she admitted that such apparel might be convenient and comfortable, but laughingly said that the infants 'looked rather like little gnomes, and that she preferred "frilly babies"'.[9] Yet she also rejected self-consciously showy clothes for children. Frilliness meant femininity, not unnecessary adornment. Cotton meant cleanliness and purity. The Duchess, suggested one account, had 'definite ideas about dressing a child, and they can be summed up in the single word Simplicity'.[10] When the Princess was a baby and toddler, she was dressed predominantly in white; when she grew older, she and her sister 'could not have been more simply dressed,' according to their governess.[11] Simplicity was linked to a sturdy, even spartan, approach: simple, sensible clothes as a feature of a simple, sensible upbringing. 'They don't wear hats at play, even on the coldest and windiest days,' wrote one commentator.[12] The Duchess's attitude seemed to rub off on her daughter who, in adolescence, 'never cared a fig' about what she wore.[13]

Such an approach seemed both patriotic and morally proper at a time when British was deemed best in the nursery, as everywhere else. At first, the Princess occupied a room at 17 Bruton Street which had been used by her mother before her marriage. Here, Lady Strathmore had made sure that 'in all the personal details that give character to a room,' the surroundings were 'typically English'.[14] After a few months, the nursery and its establishment of custodians moved to the Yorks' new residence at 145 Piccadilly, a tall, solid-looking building, later destroyed by a wartime bomb, close to Hyde Park Corner, and almost opposite St George's Hospital.

145 Piccadilly was a town house of the kind often maintained as a London base by aristocratic and other wealthy families who were happiest in the country. It was spacious (an estate agent's advertisement claimed that including servants' quarters, there were 25 bedrooms)[15] but unremarkable. When they were there, the standard of living of the King's second son and his wife was far from meagre. According to one account in 1936, staff kept at 145 Piccadilly included a steward, a housekeeper, the Duchess's personal maid, the Duke's valet, two footmen, three maids, a cook and two kitchen maids, a nurse, a nursery-maid, a boy and a night-watchman. A few years earlier, there had been an under-nurse as well.[16] Nevertheless, the Yorks' existence – cheek-by-jowl with the establishments of rich professionals, bankers and businessmen, as well as of landowners – was not unusual in aristocratic or plutocratic terms.

The photographer Lisa Sheridan first visited the Piccadilly house in the late 1920s (her mother happened to be a friend of the house-keeper). She later recalled a white terraced building, indistinguishable from those on either side of it. There was a semi-basement kitchen, 'like the giant's kitchen in a pantomime with its immense shiny copper pots and great fire-range'. The upstairs interior style reflected the taste of the Duchess more than of the Duke. Vast oil paintings, including a picture of horses, hung in heavy gilt frames in the dim, over-furnished entrance hall, alongside huge elephant tusks, mementoes of some-body's big game hunt. There was also a painted, life-size statue of a black boy.[17] An extensive garden at the back, shared with other houses, added an element of community. As the Princess grew older she was able to play on the lawns and paths with the children of the merely well-to-do, although a zoo-like atmosphere developed, as members of the public, tipped off by the press, acquired the habit of peering through the railings.[18]

Elizabeth lived in a suite of rooms at the top of the house, consisting of a day nursery, a night nursery and a bathroom linked by a landing, with wide windows looking down on the park. Here Mrs Sheridan remembered seeing the Princess, 'her pretty doll-like face . . . framed in soft silky curls'. Around her were the typical *accoutrements* of an inter-war upper-class infant's lair: a rocking horse, baby clothes hung up to dry, a nanny knitting in a rocking chair. The impression was of devotion and reassurance, but also of order, neatness and discipline; the Princess, at the crawling stage, was only allowed to play with one toy at a time.[19]

There was no question about who was in charge. The Yorks' gover-ness later aptly described the regime as 'a state within a state,' with the nanny, Clara Knight (known as 'Alla'), as ever-present benign dictator, 'a shoulder to weep on, a bosom to fall asleep on,' who 'would sit at evening in the rocker . . . mending or knitting and telling stories of "when Mummie was a little girl"'.[20] Alla was a former Strathmore retainer who had looked after the Duchess and her brother: Elizabeth Cavendish, a contemporary of the Princess, remembers her, from children's parties, as a 'formidable' figure.[21] Unmodern to a fault, she controlled the life of the Princess – health, dress and bath.

The tiny Princess, half-royal by birth, lived in her earliest years a half-royal existence. At first, much of it was spent with her parents, as they travelled restlessly around the great houses of people to whom they were related, like members of any great family. Soon, however, the requirements of royalty produced long parental absences, and the role of Alla and her assistants grew.

From babyhood, Princess Elizabeth was often in Scotland, either staying with her Strathmore (Bowes-Lyon) grandparents at Glamis Castle in Forfarshire, or with her royal ones at Balmoral Castle in Aberdeenshire. She spent much of her first summer in an ancient nursery wing at Glamis, or sleeping in the Castle garden 'to the rhythmic sound of tennis balls on hard courts where her elders played, and to the song of laden bees. And when she awoke it was to smile at her father and mother as they started off on some fishing expedition . . .' At the end of August, when Elizabeth was four months old, the Duke and Duchess of York left her in the care of the Countess of Strathmore while they went, like most of the young mothers and fathers, modern and unmodern, who were known to them, on 'a round of visits to friends'.[22]

This was the prelude to a much longer parting. Earlier in the year, the Duke of York had accepted an invitation to open the Commonwealth Parliament in the new Australian capital of Canberra. It was taken for granted both that his wife would accompany him and that their baby daughter would not. After Christmas, therefore, the Yorks took the Princess to the Strathmores' Hertfordshire home at St Paul's Walden Bury, and there they left her, for the duration of the royal tour. After they had sailed from Portsmouth early in January 1927, the Duchess wrote from on board the battle cruiser *Renown* to her mother-in-law that she had 'felt very much leaving on Thursday, and the baby was so sweet playing with the buttons on Bertie's uniform that it quite broke me up'.[23] Neither the King, nor the Queen, nor the Duke, however, would have seen anything unusual about such a trip. As Prince of Wales, George V had himself taken his wife on several foreign or imperial tours, without the encumbrance of their young children.

In any case, there was much to take the minds of the Duke and Duchess off their baby daughter. Prince Albert Frederick Arthur George, known as 'Bertie' to his family, had been made Duke of York in 1920, at the age of twenty-five. Yet he had not at that time sought a prominent royal role, and no exacting royal responsibilities had so far been asked of him. Shy and slow as a child, and the victim of a stammer since the age of seven or eight, he disliked and avoided occasions when he might be required to speak – so much so, that some had regarded him as not only reclusive, but intellectually backward. There had been some recent improvement. His marriage to Lady Elizabeth Bowes-Lyon in 1923 had increased his confidence. So too, during the months before the voyage, had a course of instruction from an Australian speech therapist. But his appearances before large audiences had been infrequent, and – except over events like weddings and births – the public had taken less interest in him and his wife than in other members of the Royal Family. 'The news-reels didn't bother them very much,' noted one commentator, a few years later, 'and the press left them pretty much alone.'[24] Australia, where the Duke was to represent his father before the people of an intensely loyal dominion, was his first major testing ground.

The tour was exacting, psychologically as well as physically, for it aroused huge public curiosity. The Yorks' itinerary involved going, via Panama, to Fiji and New Zealand before they reached Sydney. In Australia, a programme of visits took them to cities around the country, culminating in their arrival at Canberra for Bertie's painfully rehearsed, much feared speech at the opening ceremony. During the ominous build-up, the Duke and Duchess were fêted at each stop. The local press eagerly examined every available detail of the lives of the previously little-known couple, who seemed to embody the mother country, for which sentimental and nostalgic feelings remained strong. As the tour progressed, fascination increased, especially for the most humanizing detail of all: the distant and as yet inarticulate Princess. 'Wherever we go cheers are given for her as well,' Bertie wrote to his mother, '& the children write to us about her.'[25] The newspapers dubbed her 'Betty,' and she became the tour's unofficial mascot. The Duke and Duchess were soon besieged with questions about 'the World's Best Known Baby'. They were also loaded with gifts for her, each locality or association vying with its rivals to produce the most loving, ingenious and appropriate present. The Brownies of Auckland delivered a large doll, the children of Fremantle gave a miniature bed, together with a box of miniature clothes, the National Council of Women sent a gold porringer, and the Melbourne Arts and Crafts Society proudly proffered an Australian Noah's Ark, complete with kangaroos, wallabies and other antipodean survivors of the Flood. In May 1927, it was estimated that three tons of toys had so far been presented for Betty, *in absentia*. The soldier who guarded them reputedly said there were more dolls in the collection than there were men in his regiment.

At home, however, Alla's one-toy-at-a-time regime did not alter. The Princess's first day without her parents was reported by the newspapers to be just like any other. Though it was the depth of winter, her nanny took her in a pram on a two-hour walk through Mayfair into Hyde Park, where she appeared perfectly content, fast asleep, and (suitably, for the granddaughter of a King-Emperor) clutching a golliwog under the covers. Supposedly, she 'seemed to miss her mother's regular morning visit to the nursery,' though how anyone could tell was not revealed.[26]

In February, the Alla establishment joined George V and Queen Mary at Buckingham Palace, and in April they followed the Court to Windsor, where the Princess spent her first birthday. The King and Queen enjoyed the idea of being *in loco parentis* (although it involved little contact with the child) and the Queen, particularly, took it very seriously. There was a daily ritual. Every afternoon, Alla would bring Princess Elizabeth down to her grandparents, 'and the appearance at the door of a very little person in a white gown and fringed sash would be greeted by the Queen's delighted cry of "Here comes the Bambino!"'[27] Photographs and written reports of the baby's progress were sent to her parents. 'She has 4 teeth now,' the King told them in March, 'which is quite good at eleven months, she is very happy and drives in a carriage every afternoon, which amuses her'.[28] The Strathmores were able to tell of other accomplishments. During the last two months of the Yorks's absence, the Princess stayed at St Paul's Walden Bury. Here, Alla patiently taught her to enunciate the word 'Mummy'. Since, however, there was nobody to whom the word could be accurately applied, she greeted everybody she came across, including family portraits, 'with the salutation "Mummy, Mummy!"'[29]

As one writer observed later in the Princess's childhood, 'the parents who came back to her from the other end of the earth were strangers'.[30] The Duke and Duchess returned in June after six months away, laden with toys, to greet a child they barely recognized, who was almost twice the age she had been when they departed. The reunion involved a poignant little ceremony in the Grand Hall at Buckingham Palace where the King and Queen and the Earl and Countess of Strathmore had assembled with the Household staff to provide a welcoming party. The Duchess, seeing the baby in its nurse's arms, rushed forward, exclaiming 'Oh you little darling', and kissed and hugged it repeatedly.[31]

Glad to be home, flushed with the unexpected triumph of their tour, and delighted to see their daughter, the Yorks were happy to relax for a while in London after such an arduous journey. However, they did not stay still for long. Within a few weeks, they had left the capital for the shooting season – the Duke to join the Duke and Duchess of Devonshire, the Duchess to visit her parents at Glamis. At first, Princess Elizabeth stayed in London, but after another short separation, she was dispatched to Scotland, where a mother-daughter relationship was re-established. 'Elizabeth is learning to walk – very dangerous!' wrote the Duchess of York at Glamis. In September 1927, the whole family joined the King and Queen at Balmoral. Then they returned south for the autumn months, in order to settle properly into their house in Piccadilly.

IN ALL ACCOUNTS of Princess Elizabeth as a child, legend and reality are inseparable. The observations of those with direct knowledge were fed, not just by what they saw, but also by popular beliefs and idealizations, colouring the way they treated her, and shaping the stories they passed on which, in turn, fed the myths. Two themes stand out in the early tales. According to one, the Princess was an unusually bright and interesting child, as well as an exceptionally pleasing, generous, and sunny-natured one. According to the other, she was the essence of normality, and of a typically balanced yet fallible British girlhood. These contradictory versions – the ideal and the archetype – were held simultaneously and provided the frame on which every narrative of the Princess's childhood was built, including the anecdotes of those close to her. They also shaped the way the world came to see her as an adult and as a monarch.

The manufacture of a publicly known personality for the Princess began with her appearance. The world, peering into the royal perambulator, detected an ethereal quality. After a visit to the Bruton Street nursery, one early eulogizer wrote that the infant Elizabeth had 'the sweetest air of complete serenity about her. While we were talking, her nurse came in to fetch her, and the Duchess threw round her daughter's head . . . a filmy veil of gossamer, from which she looked down out of her nurse's arms smiling angelically at her mother, like a cherub out of a cloud'.[32]

Yet if the Princess's blond Botticelli curls, blue eyes and plump cheeks made it easy to cast her as an angel, it was important that she should also be seen as a mischievous one. After a Christmas party in 1927 for four hundred tenants on the Sandringham Estate, the press reported that the twenty-one-month-old apparition, wearing a white dress, silk socks and white shoes, suddenly materialized, standing upright on the table, 'chattering and bombarding the guests with crackers handed to her by her mother.'[33] There was also another version of the image of a small person bombarding big ones with harmless objects. At 145 Piccadilly, the Princess would allegedly get a small toy, such as a teddy bear or a ball, and drop it from the nursery landing down the stairwell onto visitors as they arrived at the house.[34] Other stories also emphasized that, for all the other-worldliness, the child was cheeringly imperfect. Ruth St Mawr, a friend of Lady Strathmore, told a story about taking tea at Glamis Castle when Princess Elizabeth, by then three, bounded in. 'You can't think how naughty I've been,' declared the child. 'Oh, *so* naughty, you don't know.' 'Well then tell me,' said Lady Strathmore, 'and I *shall* know.' 'No,' said Princess Elizabeth – and that was that.[35]

Normality required a pet-name and this, the press was delighted to discover, Princess Elizabeth herself provided early on. At two and a half, she was reported to be calling herself 'Tillabet'.[36] Later, this became 'Lisabet' or 'Lilliebeth,' before settling down as 'Lilibet,' the name her close family have continued to call her all her life. Normality also required a passion, and this, too, the Princess obligingly furnished in her lifelong love of horses and dogs, which could be dated to the autumn of 1928, when the Duke of York took Naseby Hall in Northamptonshire for the hunting season, and Elizabeth accompanied her parents there for much of the winter. According to one inter-war chronicler, it was at Naseby 'that Lisabet really fell in love with beautiful horses'. She enjoyed patting her father's animals, and her nurse had to watch her closely, because of her habit of running off to the stables at the slightest excuse at any time of day.[37] In addition, apparently, 'she especially loved the hounds with their nervous erect tails and their elemental eagerness to be off'.[38]

Horses and dogs had to be trained, and from a tender age, Princess Elizabeth was often portrayed in appropriate roles of command and authority in relation to them. But royal children required training too, and it was made clear, in every tale, that the Princess's mischief was never allowed to get out of hand. If Elizabeth had a sense of fun, it was also (commentators took care to point out) kept in check. 'Uncurbed without being spoilt' was how the *Sunday Dispatch* described the barely walking child in an article entitled 'The Roguish Princess'.[39] 'Roguish' was a favourite term in such accounts: it implied misbehaviour within acceptable and endearing limits. According to Alice Ring's royally sanctioned description of the Princess, published in 1930, on one occasion Elizabeth said 'My Goodness!' in the hearing of her mother. She was 'at once told that this was not pretty and mustn't be repeated'. However, if she heard an adult use the unseemly expression, 'up go her small arms in a gesture of mock amazement, and she presses her palms tightly over her mouth while her blue eyes are full of roguish laughter'.[40]

Uncurbed was never allowed to mean over-indulged. 'I don't think any child could be more sensibly bought up,' Queen Mary remarked. 'She leads such a simple life and she's always punished when she's naughty.'[41] Here was a useful moral tale, for the edification of millions. 'Once Lisbet had been naughty, for even princesses can be naughty, you know,' wrote Captain Eric Acland, author of a particularly cloying biography published when Elizabeth was twelve, 'and her mother, to punish her, refused to tell the usual bedtime story.'[42] According to another writer, if the Duchess of York was asked what her main duty was, 'she would reply, "Bringing up my children". She brings them up as she herself was brought up, with unremitting care and great practical intelligence.'[43] It was the accepted view. 'No child of Queen Elizabeth's will ever be spoilt,' the writer Stephen King-Hall summed up, at the time of George VI's Coronation.[44]

But how could any child receive so much attention, and be the object of so many admiring glances, yet not be spoilt, even allowing for parental firmness? Here was an even deeper paradox in the iconography, never satisfactorily resolved. The usual answer – and the one that dominated characterizations of the Princess until her adolescence – was that her innocence was protected, as if by wall and moat, from the corrupting effects of vulgar fame and even of excessive loyal adoration. Chocolates, china sets and children's hospital wards, even a territory in Antarctica, were named after her; the people of Newfoundland had her image on their postage stamps; songs were written in her honour, and sung by large assemblies of her contemporaries; while Madame Tussaud's displayed a wax model of her astride a pony. However, according to one chronicler in the early 1930s, 'of all this she is unconscious, it passes her completely by – and she remains just a little girl, like any other little girl . . . and passionately fond of her parents'.[45] There was also the idea of a fairy-tale insulation from the projected thoughts and fantasies of the outside world – a 'normal' childhood preserved, by an abnormal caesura, from public wonder. 'In those days we lived in an ivory tower' wrote Elizabeth's governess, many years later, 'removed from the real world'.[46]

Yet the very protection of the Princess, the notion of her as an innocent, unknowing, unsophisticated child who, but for her royal status, might be anybody's daughter, niece or little sister, helped to sustain the popular idea of her as a ray of sunshine in a troubled world, a talisman of health and happiness. This particular quality was often illustrated by tales of her special, even curative, relationship with the King, which juxtaposed youth and old age, gaiety and wisdom, the future and the past, in a heavily symbolic manner. From the time of the Yorks' Australian tour, when the Princess was fostered at Buckingham Palace, it had been observed that the ailing Monarch, whose health was becoming a matter of concern throughout the Empire, derived a special pleasure from the company of his granddaughter.

There were many accounts which brought this out. 'He was fond of his two grandsons, Princess Mary's sons,' the Countess of Airlie recalled, 'but Lilibet always came first in his affections. He used to play with her – a thing I never saw him do with his own children – and loved to have her with him'.[47] Others observed the same curious phenomenon: on one occasion, the Archbishop of Canterbury was startled to encounter the elderly Monarch acting the part of a horse, with the Princess as his groom, 'the King-Emperor shuffling on hands and knees along the floor, while the little Princess led him by the beard'.[48] When she was scarcely out of her pram, a visitor to Sandringham reported watching the King 'chortling with little jokes with her – she just struggling with a few words, "Grandpa" and "Granny"'.[49] The Princess's governess recalled seeing them together, near the end of the King's life, 'the bearded old man and the polite little girl holding on to one of his fingers'. Later, it was claimed that the King was 'almost as devoted a slave to her as her favourite uncle, the Prince of Wales'.[50]

Yet it was also stressed that she was taught to know her place. Deferential manners were an ingredient of the anecdotes, alongside the spontaneity. One guest noted that after a game of toy bricks on the floor with an equerry, she was fetched by her nurse, 'and made a perfectly sweet little curtsey to the King and Queen and then to the company as she departed'. This vital piece of royal etiquette had been perfected before her third birthday. When it was time to bid her grandfather goodnight, she would retreat backwards to the door, curtsey and say, 'I trust your Majesty will sleep well'.[51] Some accounts took the Princess's concern beyond mere politeness. For example, it was said that when the King was sick, she asked after him, and, on seeing her grandmother, 'flung herself into the Queen's arms and cried: "Lillybet to see Grandpar today?"'[52] There were also reports that when the royal landau passed down Piccadilly a shrill cry was heard from the balcony at No. 145: 'Here comes Grandpa!' – causing the crowd to roar with loyal delight.[53] There was much approval, too, for her name for the King: 'Grandpa England'.[54]

But the most celebrated aspect of the relationship concerned the Princess's prophylactic powers during the King's convalescence from a near-fatal illness in the winter of 1928–9. During this anxious time, the little girl 'acted as a useful emollient to jaded nerves,'[55] a kind of harp-playing David to the troubled Monarch's Saul.

In March 1929, the Empire learnt that the Princess, not yet three, was being encouraged to spend much of the morning with the recuperating King in his room at Craigweil House in Bognor, in order to raise his spirits. For an hour or so, she would sit with him by his chair at the window, making 'the most amusing and original comments on people and events'.[56] The King recovered, and his granddaughter was popularly believed to have played a part in bringing this about. Many years later, Princess Elizabeth told a courtier that the old Monarch's manner 'was very abrupt, some people thought he was being rude'.[57] The fact that he terrified his sons, and barked at his staff, gave the stories of the little girl's fearless enchantments an even sharper significance.

For her fourth birthday in 1930, the doting old man made Elizabeth the special gift of a pony. At this news public adoration, both of the giver and the recipient, literally overflowed. The same day, the Princess, in a yellow coat trimmed with fur, was seen walking across the square at Windsor Castle, with a band of the Scots Guards providing an accompaniment. Women waved their handkerchiefs and threw kisses. The Princess waved back, and 'her curly locks fluttered in the breeze'. The sight was too much for the crowd. People outside the Castle gate suddenly pressed forward, and swept the police officer on duty off his feet.[58]

2

THE DUCHESS OF YORK gave birth to a second child at Glamis Castle in August 1930. Although a Labour Government was now in office, traditional proprieties were once again observed – this time at even greater inconvenience to the new Home Secretary, J. R. Clynes, than to his predecessor. Summoned north for the expected event, Clynes was kept waiting for five days as a guest of the Countess of Airlie, at Cortachy Castle. He made no complaint, and seems to have enjoyed his part in the ritual. Later he described how, after the announcement, 'the countryside was made vivid with the red glow of a hundred bonfires, while sturdy kilted men with flaming torches ran like gnomes from place to place through the darkness'.[1]

The arrival of Princess Margaret Rose had several effects. One was to reinforce public awareness of her sister. The child was not a boy, the King's health remained uncertain, and the Prince of Wales showed no sign of taking a wife. A minor constitutional controversy, following the birth, helped to remind the public that Elizabeth's position was an increasingly interesting one. Although common sense indicated that, after the Prince of Wales and the Duke of York, she remained next in line, doubts were raised about whether this was really the case. Some experts argued that legally the two sisters enjoyed equal rights to the succession: there was nothing, in law, to say that they did not, and the precedence of an elder sister over a younger had never been tested. The King ordered a special investigation. The matter was soon settled, to the satisfaction of the Court, and as the Sovereign himself no doubt wished.[2]

Another effect was to give Elizabeth a companion, and the public an additional character on which to build an ever-evolving fantasy. The Yorks were now a neatly symmetrical family, the inter-war ideal. There were no more children to spoil the balance, or dilute the cast.

After the birth of Margaret Rose, 145 Piccadilly acquired a settled, tranquil, comforting air, and the image of it became a fixed point in the national and imperial psyche. When people imagined getting married and setting up a home, they thought of the Yorks. The modest, reserved, quietly proud father, the practical, child-centred mother, the well-mannered, well-groomed daughters; the ponies, dogs and open air; the servants dealing with the chores, tactfully out of sight; the lack of vanity, ambition, or doubt – all represented, for Middle England and its agents overseas, a distillation of British wholesomeness.

It did not matter that the Yorks were not 'the Royal Family' – that the Duke was not the King, or ever likely to be. Indeed, it helped that they were sufficiently removed from the ceremonial and servility of the Court to lead comprehensible lives, and for their daughters to have the kind of fancy-filled yet soundly based childhood that every boy and girl, and many adults, yearned for. At a time of poverty and uncertainty for millions, the York princesses in their J. M. Barrie-like London home and country castles stood for safety and permanence. The picture magazines showed them laughing, relaxed, perpetually hugging or stroking pets, always apart from their peers, doll-like mascots to adorn school and bedroom walls. Children often wrote to them, as if they were playmates, or sisters: little girls they already knew. Story books spun homely little tales around their lives, helping to incorporate them as imaginary friends in ordinary families.

The most dramatic attempt to appropriate them for ordinariness occurred in 1932, with the erection of a thatched cottage, two-thirds natural size, by 'the people of Wales,' as a present for Princess Elizabeth on her sixth birthday. This remarkable object made an implicit point, for no part of the United Kingdom had suffered more terrible unemployment than the mining valleys of the principality. Built exclusively by Welsh labour out of Welsh materials, it provided a stirring demonstration of the ingenuity of a workforce whose skills were tragically wasted. At the same time – loyally and movingly – its creators sought to connect the lives of the little Princess and her baby sister to those of thousands of children who inhabited real cottages. The point, however, could not be too political, and an abode, even an imitation one, intended for a princess had to be filled with greater luxuries than average families ever experienced.

Great efforts were made to ensure that it conformed to the specifications of a real home. Electric lights were installed, and the contents included a tiny radio, a little oak dresser and tiny china set, linen with the initial 'E', and a portrait of the Duchess of York over the dining-room mantelpiece. The house also contained little books, pots and pans, food cans, brooms, and a packet of Epsom salts, a radio licence and an insurance policy, all made to scale. The bathroom had a heated towel rail. In the kitchen, the reduced-size gas cooker, copper and refrigerator worked, and hot water came out of the tap in the sink.

It was scarcely a surprise present. Months of publicity preceded its completion. There was also a near-disastrous mishap. When the house was finished and in transit, the tarpaulin protecting it caught fire, and the thatched roof and many of the timbers were destroyed. Though some felt it lucky that the incendiary nature of the materials had been discovered before, and not after, the Princess was inside, the project was not abandoned. Instead, indefatigable craftsmen worked day and night to repair the damage and apply a fire-resistant coating, in time to display the renovated house at the Ideal Home Exhibition at Olympia.[3] Then it was reconstructed in Windsor Great Park for the birthday girl, and became a favourite plaything.

Whatever Elizabeth may have made of the house's message, she and her sister were soon using it for the purpose for which it was intended: to exercise and display their ordinariness. Elizabeth was 'a very neat child,' according to her governess, and the Welsh house provided an excellent opportunity to show it. The two girls spent happy hours cleaning, dusting and tidying their special home.[4] Thousands of people who had experienced a vicarious contact with royalty by inspecting the cottage when it was on public show, were later able to enjoy a series of photographs of the elfin princesses, filling the doorway of 'Y Bwthyn Bach' – the Little House – not just as children but as Peter Pan adults, miniaturized in a securely diminutive world, the perfect setting for the fantasy of 'royal simplicity'. The contrast between the oriental extravagance of the structure – fabulously costly in design, equipment, production and delivery – and the games that were to be played in it, highlighted the triumphant paradox.

It was also, of course, a *female* artefact, a point made by Lisa Sheridan, when the children proudly took her on a tour in 1936:

> In the delightful panelled living-room everything was in its proper place. Not a speck of dust anywhere! Brass and silver shone brilliantly. Everything which could be folded was neatly put away. The household brushes and the pots and pans all hung in their places. Surely this inspired toy provided an ideal domestic train-ing for children in an enchanted world ... Everything in the elegantly furnished house had been reduced, as if by magic, to those enchanting proportions so endearing to the heart of a woman. How much more so to those young princesses whose status fitted so perfectly the surroundings?[5]

Y Bwthyn Bach gave Elizabeth a Welsh dimension. A Scottish one was provided shortly afterwards by the appointment, early in 1933, of a governess from north of the border, Marion Crawford. In a sense, of course, Elizabeth was already half-Scottish, and it was the Scottish networks of the Duchess of York that had led to the appointment. However Miss Crawford belonged to a different kind of Scotland from the one known to the Bowes-Lyons, or – for that matter – to the kilt-wearing Windsor dynasty. A twenty-two-year-old recent graduate of the Moray House Training College in Edinburgh, she came from a formidable stratum: the presbyterian lower middle class.

Miss Crawford stayed with the Yorks, later the Royal Family, teach-ing, guiding and providing companionship to both girls for fourteen years, until she married in 1947, shortly before the wedding of Princess Elizabeth. Three years later, she published a detailed account of her experiences in the royal service, against the express wishes of the Palace. 'She snaked,' is how a member of the Royal Family describes her behaviour today.[6] Perhaps it was the incongruity of a woman from such a background betraying, for financial gain, the trust that had been placed in her (as her employers came to see it) which accounted for the anger that was felt. She was not the last to snake, but she was the pioneer. Marion Crawford was soon known as 'Crawfie' to the princesses: 'doing a Crawfie' became an expression for selling family secrets, especially royal ones, acquired during a period of personal service. To the modern reader, however, Miss Crawford's *Little Princesses* is a singularly inoffensive work. Composed with the help of a ghost writer in a gushing Enid Blyton, or possibly Beverley Nichols, style, it does not destroy the Never-Never-Land mythology of 145 Piccadilly, but enhances it. Love, duty and sacrifice are the currency of daily life, and everybody always acts from the best of motives. Yet the book also has perceptiveness – and the ring of authenticity. Although effusively loyal in tone, it reveals a sharp and sometimes critical eye, and opinions which were not always official ones.

It shows a character with just enough of a rebellious edge to make the subsequent 'betrayal' explicable. Until she became notorious, Crawfie and her presence at the Yorks' hearth were regarded in the press (perhaps rightly) as evidence of the Bowes-Lyon belief in no-nonsense training for young girls. According to *The Times* on the occasion of Princess Elizabeth's eighteenth birthday, Miss Crawford 'upheld through the years of tutelage the standards of simple living and honest thinking that Scotland peculiarly respects'.[7] When the Duke of York became King, she was also felt to provide a politically useful bond between the kingdoms. The most important point about Crawfie, however, which escaped public attention at the time, was that she had aspirations, both for her charges and for herself.

She was no scholar, and seemed to share the Royal Family's indifference to academic and aesthetic values. Yet she did not share its lack of curiosity, and she had a strong, indignant sense of the Court as old-fashioned and remote. She deplored what she saw as the children's ignorance of the world, and her book – perhaps this was the most infuriating thing about it – describes her personal crusade to widen the little girls' horizons. There was a Jean Brodie, charismatic aspect to Miss Crawford, both in the power of her passionate yet selfishly demanding personality (sometimes she seemed to forget who was the princess) and in her evangelical determination to make contact with life outside. Although for part of the time she had Queen Mary as an ally, it was an uphill struggle. She did, however, take the children on educational trips, and conspired to satisfy their desire to travel on the London tube; and her greatest triumph was to persuade her employers, by then King and Queen, to allow a Girl Guide Company to be set up at Buckingham Palace. She was also a woman of her age: her other ambition was to get married, something which was incompatible with her employment and – if her own account is to be believed – one which her employers could never understand.

Crawfie was not a contented person. Indeed, the self-portrait unwittingly contained in her book suggests a rather lonely and restless one, an immigrant to England and an outsider to a strange tribe whose members, though friendly, persisted in their unusual and disturbing customs. She was a taker as much as a giver. But she was interesting, intelligent and forceful. Patricia (now Lady) Mountbatten – daughter of Louis and Edwina, and a second cousin of the princesses – remembers her from Guide meetings in the Buckingham Palace gardens as a tall, attractive, highly competent woman, 'with a good personality for bringing out somebody like Princess Elizabeth, who had a stiff upper lip ingrained from birth.'[8] There seems to have developed a mutual dependence, as she became, during critical years, the princesses' confidante and friend.

PRINCESS ELIZABETH's earliest years had been spent at 145 Piccadilly with her parents, at Glamis Castle and St. Paul's Walden Bury with one set of grandparents, or at Balmoral and Sandringham with the other. In 1931, the Yorks were granted Royal Lodge, in Windsor Great Park, by the King, and in the following year they took it over as their private country residence. Thereafter, the adapted remnant of George IV's *cottage orné* designed by John Nash, with its large, circular garden, screening of trees, and air of rustic simplicity, became one of Princess Elizabeth's most familiar homes. More than anywhere, Royal Lodge provided the setting for the Yorks' domestic idyll. Summers were spent there with a minimum of staff.

From the point of view of family life, it was an advantage (not mentioned in the newspaper profiles) that the Duke had little to do. He went on the occasional overseas visit, though never again, as Duke of York, on the scale of the 1927 Australian tour; he exchanged hospitality with relatives and friends; he gardened, he rode, and he shot. With time on his hands, he was often at home during the day and able to take luncheon with his family, and to play tag or hide-and-seek with his daughters in Hamilton Gardens. Until 1936 he and his wife seemed perfectly content with the undemanding routines of a minor member of the Royal Family, of whom little was required or expected. The Duchess had been a society beauty, fêted and wooed in her youth. After contracting a surprising if elevated marriage, however, she appeared to have no ambitions beyond the settled rhythms of an unremarkable aristocratic life, and the enjoyment of her children. Though her wit and charm made her friends wherever she went, and endeared her to other members of the Royal Family, she and her husband were not a fashionable couple, and they had little contact with the café society which held such a fascination for the Prince of Wales.

Crawfie, who disapproved of some of the grander and crustier aspects of the royal way of life, repeatedly stressed in her book that the York establishment concentrated on the children. 'It was a home-like and unpretentious household I found myself in,' she wrote. Life at 145 Piccadilly, at least as seen from the perspective of the governess, revolved around the nursery landing, or around the sleeping quarters of the Duke and Duchess. 'No matter how busy the day, how early the start that had to be made,' according to Crawfie, 'each morning began with high jinks in their parents' bedroom.' This was a daily ritual which continued up to the morning of Princess Elizabeth's marriage. The day ended with a bath and a bedtime ritual, also involving parental high jinks. 'Nothing was ever allowed to stand in the way of these family sessions.'[9]

Sandwiched between morning and evening high jinks came the Princess's education – or, as many observers have wryly observed – the lack of it. After breakfast with Alla in the nursery, Elizabeth would start lessons in a little boudoir off the main drawing-room, under the supervision of her governess. Later, she would make remarks (sometimes to put nervous, successful people at their ease) about her lack of proper schooling; and it is true that, even for a princess born out of direct line of succession to the throne, her curriculum was far from exacting.[10] According to a tactfully understated assessment in the 1950s, it was 'wide rather than deep' without any forcing, or subjection to a classical discipline.[11] It was, perhaps, a misfortune that there were no peers to offer competition, or examinations to provide an incentive. Most time was spent on English, French and history.[12] Elizabeth's dependence on a single instructor for a range of subjects was a limitation, especially as the instructor's own education went no further than a training college diploma. Other future Queens of England, also born out of the direct line, had been better served. Nevertheless, in the first half of the twentieth century a home-based education for upper class girls was normal rather than exceptional – the British equivalent of binding feet.

There were two rival versions of the Yorks' approach to the education of their daughters, and we may dismiss one of them, at least in its simple form. According to the first, semi-official, account the Duchess herself closely supervised her daughters' lessons, and personally devised a timetable which concentrated on relevant subjects, such as foreign languages, scripture, geography, imperial and constitutional history. This account was the one given to the press, especially after the Abdication. According to the second, the Duchess was quite properly concerned that Elizabeth and Margaret should not regard themselves as different from any other children of their background. 'She never aimed at bringing her daughters up to be more than nicely behaved young ladies,' reflected Randolph Churchill, after the war.[13] Sometimes the two versions were combined: the best training for a royal life, it was suggested, was a non-fussy, practical education.

Both, however, agreed on one point: the Duke and Duchess were determined, in the best traditions of the British Royal Family and aristocracy, that their children should not be intellectual. According to a newspaper report, when Elizabeth was ten, a regime which involved only seven and a half hours per week in the schoolroom had been designed with a purpose: to ensure that the elder Princess should avoid becoming a 'blue-stocking', with all the terrible consequences that that term of derision implied. With the avoidance of such a fate in mind, her studies had been planned 'in consultation with the leading educationalists in the country,' and after consideration by the Cabinet.[14]

If Crawfie is to be believed, the truth was actually more mundane. Whether or not the topic was ever seriously discussed in the Cabinet Room, it caused little anxiety at 145 Piccadilly. The attitude in the York household towards education seems, in general, to have been one of genial casualness, undisturbed in the early years by any premonition of what lay ahead. Crawfie stressed this last point: perhaps seeking a justification for the lack of pedagogic rigour. Nothing seemed less likely, she insisted, than that the two girls would ever have to play an important role in their adult lives, and consequently their parents' main concern was to give them 'a happy childhood, with lots of pleasant memories stored up against the days that might come and, later, happy marriages.'[15]

If the governess had little choice but to accept the relaxed view of her employers, the same was not true of the children's formidable royal grandmother. Queen Mary – the most serious member of the Royal Family – made purposeful forays into the Piccadilly schoolroom, and was perturbed by what she found. In an attempt to improve matters, she demanded to see a schedule of lessons, urged that Princess Elizabeth should read 'the best type of children's books,' and often chose them for her. She also thought up 'instructive amusements' for the children, like a visit to the Tower of London. 'It would have been impossible for anyone so devoted to the Monarchy as Queen Mary to lose sight of the future Queen in this favourite grandchild,' recalled the Countess of Airlie.[16] This, however, was after the Abdication. Until then, the impact of the Queen's concern was limited, partly because the Duke took as little active interest in his daughters' book-learning as the Duchess.

The Duke's relaxed attitude to female education did not mean, however, that he lacked a social conscience, or sense of royal responsibility. On the contrary: a willingness to keep his own daughters socially cocooned was combined with a strong, even progressive, interest in the plight of children from the urban slums. Before becoming King, as President of the Industrial Welfare (formerly Boys' Welfare) Association, he was involved in schemes to benefit working-class youth, and he lent his name to the pioneering Duke of York's Camp – a part paternalist, part egalitarian experiment much in the spirit of the East End universities' and public schools' settlements. Each year a hundred public schools and a hundred industrial concerns were invited to send two boys each to a summer holiday camp 'where all would be on equal terms'.[17] The aim, in the words of the organizer, Robert Hyde, was to 'tame young Bolshevists,'[18] by social mingling: each side of the divide would get to know the other and appreciate its qualities. The Duke made a practice of coming for a day or two and, appropriately clad in shorts and open-necked shirt, joining in the games and sing-songs. 'Class distinction was left outside the camp boundaries,' observed an admiring journalist.[19] At the last of the camps, at Aber-geldie near Balmoral in 1939, the princesses came daily to take part. One of the happiest and most natural of pre-war royal film clips shows the four of them, parents and daughters, sitting in a throng of laughing, chanting adolescents. It was the kind of educational activity – boisterous, slapstick, communitarian, classless – that appealed to the Duke and he was proud to show it off to his daughters.

This was as close as the princesses ever got, before the war, to any proper contact with ordinary children, middle or working class, of their own age. The question of whether a wider experience might be desirable was discussed, but discarded. For several years, there was whimsical newspaper speculation that Elizabeth might be sent to a girls' boarding school. When she was seven, the press reported a rumour that – in a daring break with royal precedent – the Princess was about to be enrolled at a preparatory establishment near London, and, furthermore, that 'one of our larger public schools' would be her eventual destination.[20] There was nothing in the story, though it is conceivable that the Duchess, who had spent two terms in her own adolescence at a day school in Chelsea, may have been behind it. A few weeks after the initial report, the *Sunday Express* announced under the headline 'Will Never Go to School: Too Embarrassing,' that the Duchess of York had asked that her elder daughter should go to school, so that she would be 'brought up like any normal girl'. But after discussion with the King, Queen and Prince of Wales, and consul-tation with Cabinet ministers – according to the paper – she had been forced to back down.[21]

Such an account is supported by the recollection of Lisa Sheridan, who remembered the Duchess telling her, just before the Abdication, that 'she regretted her own daughters would not be able to go to school,' and was concerned that they should grow up naturally and unspoilt.[22] This conversation, which took place during the brief reign of Edward VIII, coincided with fresh reports of a regal veto. The new King, it was stated, had decided against a school for Elizabeth, in accordance with the wishes of his father who had always been opposed. In addition to deference to a dead Monarch, three other arguments were reckoned to have weighed with the Princess's uncle: the jealousy the choice of any particular school would cause among schools not so favoured, 'the question of who would be her schoolmates' – that is, whether she could be protected from bad influences – and, even more spuriously, her need to study different subjects from those taken by most other girls.[23] However, neither George V nor his eldest son deserve exclusive blame for the denial to the Princess of the mixed benefits of 1930s boarding school normality. Indeed, their attitude may have been an excuse. Although it would have been difficult for the Duke and Duchess to defy the Head of State, there is no reason why, after his own accession, George VI and his wife could not have reversed the earlier decision, either for their ten-year-old daughter or their six-year-old one, if they had wished to do so.

But there was one aspect of the Princess's education that was not neglected: in view of the sporting pursuits of her parents, it would have been remarkable if it had been. Surrounded from earliest childhood by horses, and by servants who trained, fed and groomed, and relatives who owned, rode and talked about them, Elizabeth, like many aristocratic little girls, became a keen equestrian. Every account of her infancy suggests that an interest in horses and ponies was almost innate. George V, player of nursery equestrian games, was one influence: it may not be coincidence that Elizabeth's early interest in horses and ponies followed her grandfather's greatest racing success, when his filly Scuttle won the 1,000 Guineas in 1928. Her first reported riding 'lesson' took place in the private riding school in Buckingham Palace Mews in January 1930, when she was three and a half, under the supervision of the Crown Equerry, Colonel A. E. Erskine.[24] It was her parents, however, who became her first serious teachers. When she was five, the Duchess led her on Peggy, the Shetland pony given by the King, to a meet of the Pytchley Hounds at Boughton Cover. For a time the stud groom at the Royal Mews took charge of the children's riding. 'The Princess will undoubtedly be a keen horsewoman when she grows up,' it was accurately predicted when she was ten.[25]

In 1938, the royal riding instructor, Horace Smith, took over and began giving the two girls twice-weekly lessons at the Palace, accompanied by his own daughter. Training included mounting exercises, like touching their toes and leaning backwards until they were lying down on their ponies' backs, to improve their balance and confidence. Smith found Elizabeth, in particular, a good and eager pupil – a conscientious listener, and keen to improve her skills. He also noticed something else: she was as interested in the business of looking after horses as in riding them; and she would ply him with questions about their feeding and management. 'I think that in those days, when she was twelve years old, her chief interest in life lay in horses,' Smith later recalled. On one occasion she told him, a sentiment often later repeated, that 'had she not been who she was, she would like to be a lady living in the country with lots of horses and dogs'.[26]

Dogs mattered almost as much as horses: a point which also did not escape royal observers of the day. As ordinary children more often owned dogs than horses, the princesses' canine interest provided, in some ways, a stronger bond. It quickly became established that not only did Elizabeth and Margaret Rose like dogs, they had a special feeling, and even an empathy, for them. Articles and books about royal caninism became a genre. '. . . [F]ew people realise the marked similarity between the unaffected sincerity that so delightfully characterizes these royal but very human children, and the cheerful contentment of their dogs,' reflected an especially liquid work called *Our Princesses and their Dogs* in 1936. 'I doubt if I have ever encountered dogs who shared with their owners a quieter or serener companionship.'[27] Photographs of the children mercilessly mothering plump corgis – the family's favourite breed – filled the picture papers.

But it was the horse world that always took precedence. With Princess Elizabeth, horses were more than an interest: they became a passion, even an obsession. Rooms and corridors, first at 145 Piccadilly, then at Buckingham Palace, were filled with an expanding collection of toy and ornamental horses, of every material and size. Not just the indulgent old King but the governess as well were cajoled into the performance of equine role-play. A favourite game was to harness Crawfie with reins, as if she were pulling a grocery cart. Then she would be patted, given a nosebag, jerked to a standstill, or instructed to paw the ground. If the weather was cold enough for her nostrils to steam, so much the better. Sometimes, however, Elizabeth would weary of this ritual. She herself would become the horse, and make 'convincing little whinnying noises'. At other times, she and her sister would sit for hours at the window at 145 Piccadilly, watching for horses in the street.[28]

Were animals a substitute for other children? Her governess, in describing such pursuits, clearly implied that they were – indeed the idea of a 'poor little rich girl' who lived a well-ordered, comfortable, but isolated life is central to her account. The two images of simplicity and loneliness are juxtaposed. On the one hand, there is a stress on the gap between the luxury people imagined royalty to enjoy, and their disciplined real lives; on the other, Crawfie often describes the yearning of the girls to be just like other children, with the same kind of fun. In her version of the princesses' childhood, bedtimes were early, treats were few, seaside holidays rare, pantomimes visited only once a year. Other children seldom came to tea. For a time, Elizabeth made 'rather special friends' with the daughter of an eminent radiologist who happened to be a neighbour, but this unusual relationship ended when the child was sent away to school. It was, according to Crawfie, difficult for the children to gain other companions. The Duke of York was a private and unassuming man who, although he did not shun social life, did not seek it either. He and his wife rarely dined out or went to the cinema or theatre, and he was perfectly content to spend the evening at the family hearth, with his wife and daughters, indulging his hobby of needlework, pursued with such diligence that, during one burst of embroidering activity, he made a dozen chair covers in *petit point* for Royal Lodge. The impression is of cosiness, but also of domestic claustrophobia.

Perhaps such a picture of seclusion was exaggerated, and related as much to Miss Crawford's home-sickness for Scotland as to the actual feelings of her charges. Meetings with the offspring of suitable parents, mostly relatives and courtiers, did occur. Elizabeth seemed to mix with them happily and naturally. Yet there seems always to have been a gulf, unavoidably imposed by convention, which stood in the way of equality. Patricia Mountbatten remembers Elizabeth coming to tea as a little girl of five or six with curly blonde hair, at her parents' London home. She recalls a child like any other – except that she attracted special interest among the adults. There was a buzz of excitement among the nannies and governesses. 'She wasn't just another child of friends of my parents. She created a little flutter.'[29] An aristocratic contemporary remembers meeting Elizabeth for the first time at his birthday party when they were both three. He had received a pedal car as a present, and his father insisted that he should let her ride in it. 'She was a princess,' he says. 'You knew she was different.'[30]

As ELIZABETH grew, interest in her increased. Visitors inspected her closely and seldom failed to remark afterwards on her beauty and poise, and on a precocious maturity achieved (so it was said) without loss of childish innocence. At the same time, a constitutionally convenient contrast was drawn between her own character, and that of her younger sister. Crawfie was later blamed for inventing this distinction, but that is unfair. Long before the publication of her book, it had been firmly implanted in the public mind. The roguishness of Elizabeth faded, especially as her destiny became apparent, and weightier qualities took over. Early in the reign of George VI, one writer compared the artistic and musical leanings of Margaret with the 'serious turn of mind' of Elizabeth, who also had an aptitude for languages. In disposition, it was noted, the elder Princess was 'quiet, unassuming and friendly, yet she has inherited a dignity which properly becomes her position.'[31] In a book published in 1939, the journalist Beverley Baxter wrote of Margaret's talents as a mimic, and Elizabeth's tendency to frown on 'her sister's instinct to burlesque, while secretly enjoying it'.[32] Margaret was presented as impish and whimsical, Elizabeth as dutiful and responsible. 'Margaret's capacity for mischief, practical joking and mimicry,' maintained a typical account in 1940, produced an elder-sister sense in Elizabeth.[33]

On one point there was unanimity: individually and together, roguish and responsible, the princesses were a credit to their parents and the nation. 'A perfectly *delicious* pair,' wrote the diplomat Miles Lampson in his diary in 1934 after seeing the two girls at Birkhall, the Georgian house above the river Muick on the Balmoral Estate, lent by the King to the Duke and Duchess of York four years earlier. 'I have seldom seen such an enchanting child as Princess Elizabeth.'[34]

Their ageing royal grandfather felt the same. 'All the children looked so nice,' he wrote after the celebration of his Silver Jubilee in July 1935, 'but none prettier than Lilibet and Margaret.'[35]

The prettiness of the royal little girls – much more than the handsomeness of the Lascelles little boys – represented youth and renewal, and became one of the symbols of the Jubilee. It was a carnival time, but also a display of recovered national confidence, after the worst of the economic crisis. At the heart of the festivities was the King who – in his proud virtue, sound political judgement, unrelenting philistinism and limited intelligence – stood for so much in an Empire that stretched around the globe: country, deity, family and social order. The crowds were hard to contain.

The nine-year-old Princess Elizabeth was photographed in a carriage with the rheumy-eyed Monarch, grandfather to his peoples as well as to the child beside him. Not since the reign of Queen Victoria, and seldom even then, had a sovereign been so revered (and never, a sceptic might have remarked, on the basis of so modest an achievement). Yet the reverence pointed backwards: Elizabeth stood for the future beyond the present reign. Her portrait appeared on Jubilee stamps, and her personality and looks were compared with those of the erect, austere figure of the Queen. Her appearance, and character, were moulded in the press accounts to fit the requirements of the hour. 'Fair-skinned, blue-eyed, with regular features,' was an appropriate assessment, 'happy-natured but serious and quietly dignified.'[36]

Observing the enthusiasm of the massed well-wishers, the King was reported to be deeply moved. An uplifting year, however, had also worn him out. On Christmas Day he delivered his crackling wireless message to subjects all over the world, but with a noticeably weak voice. Over the next few days, he walked painfully in the estate at Sandringham, stopping every hundred yards to catch his breath. In the evenings, he had just enough energy left to play with his granddaughters.[37] Elizabeth had brought cheer to George V during his illness seven years earlier: once again, she appears in the stories told about him. Lord Dawson, the King's physician, later recounted how, as the end approached, the Archbishop of Canterbury, Cosmo Lang, asked the Princess if she would like to walk with him in the garden at Sandringham. 'Yes, very much,' she supposedly replied, 'but please do not tell me anything more about God. I know all about him already.'[38] F. J. Corbett, formerly Deputy Comptroller of Supply at Buckingham Palace, wrote that the last time he saw George V was on the private golf course at Sandringham, a few days after Christmas. 'Out of the mist came the King, mounted on his white pony, Jock,' he recalled. 'Walking by the head of the pony, as if leading it along, was the little figure of Princess Elizabeth. She was taking her grandfather back to the house.'[39]

On 17 January the princesses returned to Royal Lodge. The Duke of York had his own cause for anxiety in an age before antibiotics, for the Duchess was recovering from an attack of pneumonia. They had barely got home, however, when the Duke was summoned to his father's bedside. On 20 January, the King died, surrounded by the Queen and his children. Three days later his body was brought with great solemnity to London, and laid in state in the Palace of Westminster, where hundreds of thousands of mourners filed past. Four officers of the Brigade of Guards stood at the corners of the catafalque. On the last night, these were replaced by the dead King's four sons, including his successor and the Duke of York, each in uniform. Princess Elizabeth was taken by her mother to witness this extraordinary vigil, and to contemplate the coffin of her 'Grandpa England'. On 29 January, she attended the funeral at Windsor.

The accession of Princess Elizabeth's young, popular, forward-looking Uncle David as Edward VIII revived the monarchical excitement of the Jubilee. Such an event brings turmoil at Court, similar to the ferment at No. 10 Downing Street caused by the change of a Prime Minister. The hierarchy is turned upside down. Established officials fear for their jobs, or wonder whether the time has come to retire from them. The transition from the predictable George V to his febrile son was a particularly traumatic break, and it sent a tremor through the ranks of the old courtiers. Ancient customs were abandoned, rules and formalities were impatiently relaxed. The Queen was dispatched to live in Marlborough House, and unexpected faces appeared at the Palace.

The new reign also focused attention, with added intensity, on the Yorks. On the margins of the main performance, they continued to enjoy an adequate privacy. A few weeks into the new reign, Harold

Nicolson, official biographer of George V, spoke to the Duchess of York at the house of a mutual friend. He talked to her for some time, without recognizing her.[40] However, such anonymity could not last long, for the death of the old King, and the persistent bachelorhood of his replacement, brought the Duke of York a step closer to the throne. It also aroused a new kind of interest in his elder daughter. There was still no publicly acknowledgeable reason for expecting Elizabeth ever to become Queen. Yet her place in the line of succession had become much more than a statistic. It began to give rise to speculation, and romantic projection.

What if the King never married? In the run-up to the Coronation, such a possibility was tentatively aired. One commentator suggested that a female Sovereign would be rapturously welcomed, and argued that this in itself was a reason why meddlers into the King's private affairs should not seek to push him into matrimony. 'They do not realise how many of their fellow-subjects would, however respectfully, feel half sorry at such an event, however auspicious. It might deprive us of Elizabeth II.'[41] A similar thought may have occurred to Archbishop Lang, who had discussed (or refrained from discussing) theology with the Princess at Sandringham in January, and who stayed as a guest of the Yorks at Birkhall in the summer. At a time when the new King was becoming a serious worry, he was reassured by what he saw. 'The children – Lilliebet, Margaret Rose and Margaret Elphinstone – joined us,' he recorded. 'They sang some action-songs most charmingly. It was strange to think of the destiny which may be awaiting the little Elizabeth, at present second from the Throne. She and her lively little sister are certainly most entrancing children.'[42]

Yet, at first, life for 'the little ladies of 145 Piccadilly' did not alter. It may have been a symptom of her upward mobility that a marble portrait bust of Princess Elizabeth was commissioned in the spring of 1936. Over the next two years, Miss Crawford accompanied the child no fewer than eighteen times to the studio of the Hungarian sculptor Zsigmond Strobl in Pembroke Walk. Lajos Lederer, a Hungarian journalist employed to make conversation with her during these tedious sessions, recalled her as highly talkative, and extremely knowledgeable on the subject of thoroughbred horses.[43] Otherwise, the only direct effect on the princesses of the accession seemed to be that they saw less of their uncle, previously one of the Yorks' few frequent callers. The Duke and Duchess, though aware of gathering clouds, continued to ride, garden and embroider, much as before. Lisa Sheridan, visiting their London house before they left for Scotland, was led by a footman into the garden, where she found Princess Elizabeth and her mother feeding a family of ducklings which had wandered in through the railings from the adjoining park.[44]

There was no immediate mention of Wallis Simpson. When, eventually the King's American companion was invited to tea at Royal Lodge, nothing was said about the significance of the visit. But Uncle David seemed to have lost interest in his nieces.[45] For some time, there had been 'King-tattle' – gossip which, as one loyalist claimed indignantly, 'rages without respect to decency and perhaps probability,' but which did not get into print.[46] The reason was not so much the laws of libel, as the fear of breaking a taboo. Editors and proprietors calculated that the opportunity was not worth the short-term boost in sales. 'No respectable paper would have thought it good circulation policy to print scandalous news about the Royal Family,' observed the anti-monarchist editor of the *New Statesman*, Kingsley Martin, afterwards. 'It would no doubt have sold for the moment, but it would have led to a storm of protest from readers.'[47] There was also a gap between the business side of running newspapers – whose circulation policy made use of incentives like free gifts and insurance policies to attract readers – and the editorial side, which held aloof. 'Editors were a traditional lot,' says Sir Edward Pickering, then on the *Mirror*, and later a leading editor and newspaper director. 'They didn't look on circulation in the way they do today. They felt themselves above all that.'[48] On this occasion they were also afraid of a backlash, in view of the popularity of a Monarch who, as Malcolm Muggeridge put it, 'was idolized as few men outside the Orient ever have been'.[49]

Yet the gossip was pervasive, the more virulent because of the gap between what those in the King's circle knew and the messages of the headlines and newsreels. 'Those who most strenuously maintained a decorous loyalty in public,' recalled Martin, 'were the most avaricious of scandal about the Monarchy in private.'[50] Princess Elizabeth may have been ignorant of what was going on, and the Duke and Duchess never spoke of it, but according to Crawfie, 'it was plain to everyone there was a sudden shadow over the house'.[51]

The whole Royal Family, together with the whole political and Church Establishment, and many ordinary people, were shocked and appalled by the prospect of an abdication, which seemed to strike at the heart of the constitution. But nowhere was it viewed with greater abhorrence than at 145 Piccadilly. According to his official biographer, the Duke of York viewed the possibility, and then the likelihood, of his own succession with 'unrelieved gloom'.[52] The accounts of witnesses suggest that this is a gross understatement: desperation and near-panic would be more accurate. To succeed to a throne you neither expected nor wanted, because of the chance of birth and the irresponsibility of a brother! Apart from the accidents of poverty and ill health, it is hard to think of a more terrible and unjust fate.

Alan ('Tommy') Lascelles, assistant private secretary to Edward VIII and later private secretary to George VI, wrote privately that he feared Bertie would be so upset by the news, he might break down.[53] There were lurid stories: that the Duke of York had refused to succeed, and that Queen Mary had agreed to act as Regent for Princess Elizabeth.[54] Rumours circulated in the American press that the Duke was epileptic (and that Princess Margaret was deaf and dumb).[55] There was also a whispering campaign, in which Wallis Simpson played a part, that he had 'a slow brain' which did not take on ideas quickly and that he was mentally unfit for the job.[56]

On 27th October, when Mrs Simpson obtained a decree nisi, the shadow darkened. The Duke braced himself for the catastrophe, as he saw it, that was about to befall his family and himself. 'If the worst happens & I have to take over,' he wrote, with courage, to a courtier on 25 November, 'you can be assured that I will do my best to clear up the inevitable mess, if the whole fabric does not crumble under the shock and strain of it all.'[57] Meanwhile, Crawfie and the children took refuge from the atmosphere of tension by attending swimming lessons at the Bath Club, with the Duke and Duchess sometimes turning up to watch.[58]

A week later, the press's self-imposed embargo on 'King-tattle' broke, and the headlines blazoned the name of Mrs Simpson. The Royal Archives contain a chronicle, written by Bertie, which shows the extent of his misery, bordering on hysteria, as he awaited what felt like an execution. In it, he describes a meeting with his mother on December 9th, when the Abdication had become inevitable, and how 'when I told her what had happened I broke down and sobbed like a child'. There are few more poignant testimonies in the annals of the modern Monarchy than George VI's account of the occasion he most feared, but could do nothing to prevent:

> 'I ... was present at the fateful moment which made me D's successor to the Throne. Perfectly calm D signed 5 or 6 copies of the instrument of Abdication & then 5 copies of his message to Parliament, one for each Dominion Parliament. It was a dreadful moment & one never to be forgotten by those present ... I went to R.L. [Royal Lodge] for a rest ... But I could not rest alone & returned to the Fort at 5.45. Wigram was present at a terrible lawyer interview ... I later went to London where I found a large crowd outside my house cheering madly. I was overwhelmed.'[59]

A kind of fatalism took over the Duke, now the King, as the Court which had surrounded – and sought to protect and restrain – his brother, enveloped him, guiding him through the ceremonies of the next few days. There was nothing he could do, except what he was told, and nothing for his family to do except offer sympathy. According to Crawfie's account, the princesses hugged their father before he left 145 Piccadilly, 'pale and haggard,' for the Privy Council in the uniform of an Admiral of the Fleet.[60] To Parliament and the Empire, and the man now called Duke of Windsor, the Abdication Crisis was over. But for King George VI and, though she did not yet appreciate it, his elder daughter, Heiress Presumptive to the Throne, it had just begun.

3

SIXTY YEARS LATER, it is still hard to assess the impact of the Abdication of Edward VIII. Arguably it had very little. In the short run, politics was barely affected; there was no last minute appeal by the resigning Monarch for public support, as some had feared there might be; no 'King's party' was put together to back him. Indeed, the smooth management of the transition was a cause for congratulation, and was taken to show the resilience of the Monarchy, and the adaptability of the constitution. Even social critics regarded it as evidence of English establishment solidarity. 'To engineer the abdication of one King and the enthronement of another in six days,' wrote Beatrice Webb, 'without a ripple of mutual abuse within the Royal Family or between it and the Government, or between the Government and the Opposition, or between the governing classes and the workers, was a splendid achievement, accepted by the Dominions and watched by the entire world of foreign states with amazed admiration.'[1] Nevertheless, it has always been treated as a turning point, and in an important sense it was one. It broke a spell.

In the past, public treatment of the private behaviour of members of the Royal Family had contained a double standard. Since the days of Victoria and Albert, the personal life of royalty had been regarded as, by definition, irreproachable; while at the same time occasionally giving cause for disapproval or hilarity – as in the case of Edward VII when Prince of Wales, and his elder son, the Duke of Clarence. Not since the early nineteenth century, however, had it been a serious constitutional issue. The Abdication made it one – giving to divorce, and to sexual misconduct and marital breakdown, a resonance in the context of royalty, which by the 1930s it was beginning to lose among the upper classes at large. At the same time the dismissal of a King provided a sharp reminder that British monarchs reigned on sufferance, and that the pomp and sycophancy counted for nothing if the rules were disobeyed. During the crisis, there was talk of the greater suitability for the throne of the Duke of Kent – as if the Monarchy was by appointment. It came to nothing, but the mooting of such a notion indicated what the great reigns of the past hundred years had tended to obscure – that Parliament had absolute rights, and that the domestic affections of the Royal Family were as much a part of the tacit contract between Crown and people as everything else.

In theory, the British Monarchy was already, and had long been, little more than a constitutional convenience. How could it be otherwise, with a Royal Family whose position had so frequently depended on parliamentary buttressing, or on a parliamentary decision to pass over a natural claimant in favour of a more appropriate minor branch? 'If there was a mystic right in any one,' as Walter Bagehot put it dryly in 1867, 'that right was plainly in James II.'[2] Yet, in practice, there had been accretions of sentiment and loyalty which had allowed the obscure origins of the reigning dynasty to be forgotten. As a result, a traditional right or legitimacy had replaced a 'divine' one, and a great sanctity had attached to laws of succession unbroken for more than two centuries. The Abdication cut through all this like a knife – taking the Monarchy back as far as 1688, when Parliament had deprived a King of his throne on the grounds of his unfitness for it.

On that occasion, the official explanation was that James II had run away – though in reality there were other reasons for wishing to dispose of a monarch who caused political and sectarian division. In 1936, the ostensible cause of the King's departure was his refusal to accept the advice of his ministers that he could not marry a divorced woman. Yet the Government's position was also regarded as a moral, and not just a technical or legalistic one. The King's relationship with Mrs Simpson was seen as symptomatic. The nation, as one commentator put it, took a dim view of tales of frivolity, luxury and 'an un-English set of *nonceurs*', associated with the new King and minded seeing its throne 'provide a music-hall turn for low foreign newspapers'.[3] Although the decision to force Edward VIII to choose between marriage and his crown was a reluctant one, it was accompanied by a hope and belief that his successor – well-married, and with a family life that commanded wide approval – would set a better example.

But the Monarchy would never be the same again. 'All the King's horses and all the King's men,' Jimmy Maxton, leader of the left-wing Independent Labour Party, reminded the House of Commons, 'could not put Humpty-Dumpty back again.'[4] Not only was the experience regarded, by all concerned, as chastening: there was also a feeling that, though the Monarchy would survive, it had been irrevocably scrambled. Even if George VI had possessed a more forceful character, the circumstances of his accession would have taken from the institution much of its former authority. As it was, the Monarchy could never again be (in the words of a contemporary writer) 'so socially aggressive, so pushy' as under George V;[5] nor could it be so brash as under Edward VIII, whose arrival 'hatless from the air,' in John Betjeman's words, had signalled a desire to innovate. After the Abdication, George VI felt a need to provide reassurance, and to behave with a maximum of caution, as if the vulgar lifting of skirts in the autumn of 1936 had never happened. Yet there could be no simple return to the old position of the Monarch as morally powerful arbitrator, a role played by George V as recently as 1931. Under George VI, royal interventions, even minor ones, diminished. The acceptance of a cypher-monarchy, almost devoid of political independence, began in 1936.

If the Abdication was seen as a success, this was partly because of an accurate assessment that the genetic dice had serendipitously provided a man who would perform the functions of his office in the dutifully subdued way required of him. Indeed, not only the disposition of the Duke of York but the familial virtues of both himself and his wife had been a key element in the equation. The point had been made by Edward VIII in his farewell broadcast, to soften the blow of his departure, when he declared that his brother 'has one matchless blessing, enjoyed by so many of you and not bestowed on me – a happy home with his wife and children.'[6] It was also stressed by Queen Mary, when she commended her daughter-in-law as well as her second son to the nation. 'I know,' she said with feeling and with meaning, 'that you have already taken her children to your hearts.'[7] Everybody appreciated that if the next in line had happened to be a footloose bachelor or wastrel, the outcome might have been very different. As it was, the Duke of York – despite, but perhaps also because of, his personal uncertainties – turned out to be well suited to the difficult task of doing very little conscientiously: a man, in the words of a contemporary eulogizer, 'ordinary enough, amazing enough, to find it natural and sufficient all his life to know only the sort of people a Symbol King ought to know,' and, moreover, one who 'needs no private life different from what it ought to be.'[8]

To restore a faith in the Royal Family's dedication to duty: that was George VI's single most important task. There was a sense of treading on eggshells, and banishing the past. As the Coronation approached, the regrettable reason for the King's accession was glossed over in the souvenir books, and delicately avoided in speeches. The monarchist historian Sir Charles Petrie observed a few years later that there was a tendency to forget all about it, 'and particularly has this been the case in what may be described as official circles'.[9] It was partly because the memory of the episode was acutely painful to the King and Queen, as well as to Queen Mary, but it was also because of the embarrassment Edward VIII's abdication caused to the dynasty, and the difficulty of incorporating an act of selfishness into the seamless royal image. Burying the trauma, however, did not dispose of it, and the physical survival of the Duke and Duchess of Windsor – unprotected by a Court, and often teetering on the brink of indiscretion or indecorum – provided a disquieting shadow, reminding the world of an alternative dynastic story.

By contrast, the existence of 'the little ladies of 145 Piccadilly' gave the new Royal Family a trump card. If, in the eyes of the public, the Duchess of Windsor was cast as a seductress, the little ladies offered cotton-clad purity, innocence and, in the case of Princess Elizabeth, hope. It greatly helped that her virtues, described by the press since babyhood, were already well-known. What if she had inherited her uncle's characteristics instead of her father's? Fortunately the stock of attributes provided by the sketch-writers did not admit of such a possibility. The ten-and-a-half-year-old Heiress Presumptive, it was confidently observed, possessed 'great charm and a natural unassuming dignity'. The world not only already knew, but already loved her, and hoped that one day she would 'rule the world's greatest Empire' as Queen.[10]

The discovery that she had become a likely future Monarch, instead of somebody close to the throne with an outside chance of becoming one, seems to have been absorbed by Princess Elizabeth gradually. Although her father's accession, and the elimination of doubt about the equal rights of royal daughters, placed her first in line, it was not yet certain that she would ever succeed. When Princess Alexandrina Victoria of Kent was told of her expectations at almost precisely the same age in March 1830, she was reported by her governess to have replied 'I will be good'. According to Lady Strathmore, when Princess Elizabeth received the news, she 'was ardently praying for a brother'.[11] It was still imaginable: the Queen was only thirty-six at the time of the Coronation in May 1937, and shortly before it a rumour spread that she was pregnant.[12] Increasingly, however, a view of the future with Princess Elizabeth as Monarch was widely accepted. There was even some speculation that Elizabeth might be given the title of Princess of Wales.[13] According to her sister, the change of status was something they knew about, but did not discuss. 'When our father became King,' recalls Princess Margaret, 'I said to her, "Does that mean you're going to be Queen?" She replied, "Yes, I suppose it does." She didn't mention it again.'[14]

There was also the matter of where they lived. According to Crawfie, Princess Elizabeth reacted with horror when she was told that they were moving to Buckingham Palace. 'What – you mean for ever?' According to Princess Margaret, the element of physical disruption was limited. 145 Piccadilly was only a stone's throw from Buckingham Palace, and they had often gone over to see their grandparents, and to play in the garden.[15] Perhaps the distrust was more in the mind of the governess, who likened setting up home in the Palace to 'camping in a museum'.[16] The living quarters were, in any case, soon domesticated after the long era of elderly kings and queens. Elizabeth's menagerie of toy horses acquired a new setting; and a room overlooking the Palace lawns, which had briefly been her nursery in 1927, was established as a schoolroom.

More important than the change of location was the ending of a way of life. In the months before the Coronation, public attention became unrelenting. Outside the railings at Buckingham Palace, a permanent crowd formed. Inside them, it was impossible to keep up the illusion of being an ordinary family. At 145 Piccadilly, there had been few visitors, most of whom were personal friends. At the Palace, the King had to see visitors or take part in functions for much of the day, and the Queen was busy every afternoon. Before, the little girls had been able to take walks in the park and play with the children of neighbours. At the Palace, royal headquarters of an Empire, there were no neighbours and different standards applied. A famous anecdote illustrated the change. Princess Elizabeth discovered that merely by walking in front of a sentry on ceremonial duty, she could make him present arms; and having made the discovery, she could not resist walking backwards and forwards to see it repeated.[17]

There was a sense of constraint, as well as of power. According to Lajos Lederer, the accession brought an immediate change to Princess Elizabeth's previously relaxed sittings for Strobl. A detective now accompanied her everywhere, a policeman was always outside, and she 'no longer referred to Mummy and Papa, but spoke of the King and Queen'.[18] The Queen seems to have been responsible for taking customary formalities seriously, and seeing that her children did so too. According to Dermot Morrah (a trusted royal chronicler), she insisted 'that even in the nursery some touches of majesty were not out of place, an argument that had the full approval of Queen Mary'.[19] One 'touch of majesty' involved the serving of nursery meals by two scarlet-liveried footmen. In addition, though nursery food was mainly 'plain English cooking,' the menu, for some reason, was in French.[20]

The biggest strain for the Royal Family, however, was the almost intolerable pressure placed upon the new King as he came to terms with his unsought and unwelcome role. 'It totally altered their lives,' according to Lady Mountbatten. 'To begin with, the King would come home very worried and upset.'[21] George VI's speech impediment, always a handicap, became a nightmare, and every public appearance a cause of suffering. Although British journalists tactfully avoided mentioning it, foreign ones were less reticent. To the American press, suspicious that the real reason for the Abdication was Mrs Simpson's American nationality, he remained 'the stuttering Duke of York'.[22] The Queen had always taken pleasure from public occasions, and continued to display a much-admired serenity: but the King at first seemed so gauche and unhappy that doubts were raised about whether he could get through his Coronation.[23]

HE MANAGED it none the less. In the early spring of 1937, British newspapers which had loyally kept silent about Mrs Simpson, now loyally built up George VI as a 'George V second edition'.[24] Yet there was a sense of him not just as the substitute but also as a reluctant Monarch. Kingsley Martin summed up the mood thus, apostrophizing the thoughts of a supposedly typical member of the public: 'We would still prefer to cheer Edward, but we know that we've got to cheer George. After all, it's Edward's fault that he's not on the throne, and George didn't ask to get there. He's only doing his duty, and it's up to us to show that we appreciate it.'[25] Martin noted a feeling of relief and sympathy, as much as of rejoicing, and of healing a personal wound.

The Coronation itself had a wider function than the consecration of a new King. It was also Britain putting its best face to the world – the more urgently so because of the international crisis which over-shadowed the royal one. Many commentators, viewing the celebration with its hotch-potch of religion, nostalgia, mumbo-jumbo and military display, saw it simultaneously as a reminder to potential aggressors of British imperial might and a reaffirmation of British freedom. For such purposes, the Empire was unblinkingly described as if it were a democratic, almost a voluntary, association.[26]

Comparisons were proudly drawn between the symbols of liberty parading through the streets of London, and the choreographed vul-garities of European fascism. One fervent royalist saw George VI's Coronation as 'a pageant more splendid than any dictators can put on: beating Rome and Nuremberg hollow at their own bewildering best, and with no obverse side of compulsion or horror'.[27] The anthro-pologist Bronislaw Malinowski reckoned it a sound investment, as 'a ceremonial display of the greatness, power and wealth of Britain,' generating 'an increased feeling of security, of stability, and the perma-nence of the British Empire'.[28] Even the Left was impressed. Kingsley Martin agreed with the view that the British Establishment had upstaged Goebbels – and suggested that the propaganda purpose of the procession and festivities was to show that the Empire was still as strong and united as in 1914, and that Britain suffered from less class conflict than any other nation.[29]

Much depended on the central actor, who made little secret of his deep anxiety about the whole proceeding. Afterwards the King told the former Prime Minister, Ramsay MacDonald, that he had been so dazed by fear for much of the ceremony that he was unaware of what was happening.[30] However, the Westminster Abbey service went without a hitch, and the Monarch performed his part in it with appropriate gravitas. 'He carried himself well,' judged Chips Channon, who witnessed the ceremony as one of several thousand MPs, peers and other dignitaries in the congregation.[31]

A more privileged position among the spectators was given to the two princesses, who sat in the royal box with Queen Mary. For Elizabeth, particularly, the day was an important part of her education. Her governess prepared her for it by reading her Queen Victoria's account of her own Coronation, written exactly a century before, which began, 'I was awoke by the guns in the Park and could not get much sleep afterwards on account of the people, bands etc.' According to Crawfie, the elder princess took such a deep interest that she became 'one of the greatest living experts on Coronations'.[32] The girls rode to the Abbey in a glass coach. Chips Channon looked on as they 'whipped their robes on to their left arms as they had been shown, pushing up their frocks with the same movement and showing bare legs above socks'.[33] During the three-hour ceremony, Elizabeth watched intently as the Archbishop of Canterbury performed the complex rites, and her father, with the utmost difficulty, repeated the words 'All this – I promise to do'.[34]

For any child to view the Coronation at close quarters was a memorable experience: only a handful had the opportunity. For the Heiress Presumptive to see her own parents crowned, and to take part in the procession, must have been awesome. What did she think and feel? The Royal Library contains her own answer – an essay, both vivid and prosaic, written in pencil on lined paper just after the event, and carefully tied with pink ribbon. On the cover is inscribed, in neat red crayon, the words:

The Coronation
12th May; 1937
To Mummy and Papa
In Memory of Their Coronation
From Lilibet
By Herself
An Account of the Coronation

It describes how she was woken at five in the morning by the band of the Royal Marines outside her window (much as her great-great grandmother had been woken by the guns in the Park), and how, draped in an eiderdown and accompanied by her nurse-maid Bobo MacDonald, 'we crouched in the window looking onto a cold, misty morning'. After breakfast ('we did not eat very much as we were too excited') they got dressed and

> showed ourselves to the visitors and housemaids. Now I shall try and give you a description of our dresses. They were white silk with old cream lace and had little gold bows all the way down the middle. They had puffed sleeves with one little bow in the centre. Then there were the robes of purple velvet with gold on the edge.
>
> We went along to Mummy's bedroom and we found her putting on her dress. Papa was dressed in a white shirt, breeches and stockings, and over this he wore a crimson satin coat. Then a page came and said it was time to go down, so we kissed Mummy, and wished her good luck and went down. There we said Goodmorning to Aunt Alice, Aunt Marina and Aunt Mary with whom we were to drive to the Abbey. We were then told to get into the carriage . . . At first it was very jolty but we soon got used to it.

Princess Elizabeth describes the procession down the Mall, along Whitehall, to Westminster Abbey, and the walk up the aisle with her family, before she went up into the royal box with Queen Mary:

> Then the service began.
> I thought it all <u>very</u>, <u>very</u> wonderful and I expect the Abbey did, too. The arches and beams at the top were covered with a sort of haze of wonder as Papa was crowned, at least I thought so.

When Mummy was crowned and all the peeresses put on their coronets it looked wonderful to see arms and coronets hovering in the air and then the arms disappear as if by magic. Also the music was lovely and the band, the orchestra and the new organ all played beautifully.

What struck me as being rather odd was that Grannie did not remember much of her own Coronation. I should have thought that it would have stayed in her mind for ever.

At the end the service got rather boring as it was all prayers. Grannie and I were looking to see how many more pages to the end, and we turned one more and then I pointed to the word at the bottom of the page and it said "Finis". We both smiled at each other and turned back to the service.

... When we got back to our dressing-room we had some sandwiches, stuffed rolls, orangeade and lemonade. Then we left for our long drive.

On leaving the Abbey we went along the Embankment, Northumberland Avenue, through Trafalgar Square, St. James's St. Piccadilly, Regent St. Oxford St. with Selfridge's lovely figures, through Marble Arch, through Hyde Park, Hyde Park Corner, Constitution Hill, round the Memorial and into the courtyard.

Then we went up to the corridor to see the Coach coming in. Then Mummy and Papa came up and said "Goodmorning" and were congratulated. Then we all went on to the Balcony where millions of people were waiting below. After that we all went to be photographed in front of those awful lights.

When we sat down to tea it was nearly six o'clock! When I got into bed my legs ached terribly. As my head touched the pillow I was asleep and I did not wake up till nearly eight o'clock the next morning.[35]

PRINCESS ELIZABETH was eleven at the time of the Coronation, and it was an initiation for her, as well as for her parents. The day was not far off, as one writer put it in the royalty idiom of the time, when she would move out of childhood 'into a swifter current of life.'[36] Pretty and pubescent, she attracted nearly as much attention as the King and Queen during the two months of state drives, official tours and youth displays that followed. Although she continued to be dressed as a little girl, there was an increase in the number of grand occasions in which she was involved. There was also a sudden serious-ness about equipping her for future duties.

One new initiative was the establishment of a Girl Guide company at the Palace, to which a Brownie pack was attached, with the specific purpose of providing the two princesses with a training ground. Based on a romantic myth of imperial kinship, the Scouts and Guides were at their zenith, and several members of the Royal Family had honorific titles within the movement. The Buckingham Palace Company met on Wednesday afternoons and gathered together about twenty children of friends and vetted acquaintances – some, like the royal princesses, taught at home by governesses, others attending London day schools. The Guides were grouped in three patrols. Princess Elizabeth was second-in-command to Patricia Mountbatten, who was a few years older, in the Kingfisher patrol. In winter they met in one of the vast rooms in Buckingham Palace, in the summer in the gardens. There were also trips to Windsor, involving the normal activities of Girl Guides everywhere, though in an abnormal setting: tracking, bird watching, trekking with a hand-cart, cooking sausages and 'dampers' (flour balls on sticks) over a campfire. At the Palace, the long corridors were used for signalling practice.

Princess Elizabeth received no special treatment, and mixed in well with the other girls. According to Lady Mountbatten, she was 'a very efficient and capable deputy,' already with an air of authority, and popular in the Company, 'nice, easy to deal with, you'd want her as your best friend'.[37] Another member of the Company, Elizabeth Cavendish, confirms the impression of the Heiress Presumptive as a highly competent Girl Guide, who took the various activities and rituals seriously, and did well at them.[38] When a Scottish dancer came to give them special instruction, Princess Elizabeth showed a particular proficiency at dancing Highland reels.

The picture is of a conventional, unquestioning child, making the most of what was presented to her. Yet if Princess Elizabeth was not singled out, there was something different about her. 'She was very aware that how she behaved in public was very important,' says Lady Mountbatten. 'For instance, she couldn't burst into tears. If she hurt her knee she knew she must try not to cry.'[39] The Company Captain was a Miss Synge, held in awe by the girls, with Miss Crawford

THE FLOWERS AND THE PRINCESSES

Punch, 28th April 1937

assisting. Some of the Guides, Patricia Mountbatten and Camilla Wallop (later Lady Rupert Nevill), for instance, became lifelong friends.

It was not just cut knees. Incidents in the Kingfisher patrol were not, in general, leaked or reported. However, other events in Princess Elizabeth's life now were, as the press, less intrusive than later but no less curious, sought to cater for a huge public appetite for details about the royal children's lives. The princesses might not be able to cry over a minor mishap, but grazes and slight colds often got into the papers just the same. Even before their teens, public appearances had become performances. If the royal children were taken to the theatre, the newspapers automatically treated them as the main attraction – reporting every movement or gesture next day. Sometimes the theatre management, delighted by the privilege of entertaining royalty, would shower honours on them, and the spotlight would be turned in their direction. When the Heiress Presumptive attended the 1937 Christmas production of 'Where the Rainbow Ends' at the Holborn Empire, along with fifteen hundred other children, everybody was asked to stand and sing a specially composed children's verse of the National Anthem.[40] 'Normal' expeditions and natural behaviour were difficult.

The birthday of Princess Elizabeth, meanwhile, became a national event. Birthday presents were listed even in the serious newspapers, together with details of the guests and of how the anniversary was being celebrated. Stimulated by these public announcements, well-wishers would gather wherever the Princess happened to be, to cheer her and convey greetings, and she would be required to appear, and politely acknowledge them.[41] She also became the recipient of a flow of unsolicited mail, often from children in disaster areas, like Chinese orphans fleeing from the Japanese.

Some aspects of the princesses' lives did not greatly alter. The family continued to come together for weekends at Royal Lodge, where their existence remained much as it had been before. The press made much of the 'simplicity' of life at the Lodge, although actually the Royal Family enjoyed every luxury, opportunity for recreation, and service that anybody could wish for. Still, it was possible to enjoy a degree of informality. Here they could enjoy, if not simple living, then the kind of rustic domesticity which had been the greatest pleasure of the

Duke and Duchess of York before the upheaval, in the company of horses and dogs unconscious of rank, with grooms, stable boys and kennel hands to look after, handle and talk about them. Princess Elizabeth's ponies had names like Peggy and Comet; the dogs included corgis, labradors and a Tibetan lion dog, and had names like Dookie, Spark, Flash, Scruffy, Mimsey and Stiffy. The public took a keen interest in these animals. 'Dookie is unquestionably the "character" of the princesses' delightful canine family,' declared one authority in 1942.[42] On Sundays, the girls and their parents attended services at St George's Chapel or the Chapel Royal in the grounds of Royal Lodge; on Saturdays, and other days during holidays, the princesses went riding in the morning. Sometimes they walked in Windsor Forest, cycled in the royal gardens at Frogmore or swam in an outdoor pool at the Lodge. All that was lacking was the company of other children of whom they saw as little, or less, than at Buckingham Palace.[43]

Juvenile guests were rare. However, the King and Queen had to entertain official, and especially foreign, visitors who were invited to stay with increasing frequency as fears about the international crisis grew. According to Crawfie, Princess Elizabeth began to take an interest in politics at about this time, 'and knew quite a bit of what was going on in the world outside'.[44] She certainly had a unique vantage point compared with most other children of her age. In one month in 1938, four kings, a regent and a crown prince called on her parents, mainly on trips to London to rally support in defence of their countries. Visitors to Windsor early in the reign included the newly appointed American Ambassador, Joe Kennedy, and his wife Rose, who stayed for a weekend in April 1938. Rose Kennedy was moved by her brief contact with British royalty, especially its younger members. She recorded in her diary that she 'found it a great conversational convenience' that her own large brood included two children, Teddy and Jean, who were about the same ages as the princesses. During her stay, she watched out for the royal daughters, much as one might look out for rare and exotic birds when visiting their habitat, and she was not disappointed. While walking in the park surrounding the Castle, she and Joe 'ran into Princess Elizabeth hiding behind the shrubs. She had on a pink coat and was hatless and she smiled at us'. The Kennedys saw her again over luncheon, when

Elizabeth and Margaret appeared together, clad identically in rose dresses with checked blouses, red shoes with silver-coloured buckles, white socks and necklaces of coral and pearl. Elizabeth, not quite twelve, was placed next to the wicked old envoy, to his saturnine delight. After the meal, the princesses were required to accompany their parents and the ambassadorial couple as they walked 'very informally' over to Frogmore.[45]

Learning how to handle distinguished guests was one important part of an Heiress's education, and was soon extended. Shortly after the Kennedy visit, Princess Elizabeth was promoted from white socks to silk stockings, receiving a box from her mother as a birthday present.[46] She started to attend the huge, thousands-strong, garden parties held annually at Buckingham Palace. She also began occasionally to take a leading role at small-scale semi-public events, presenting rosettes at children's pony shows, and cups and shields to children at the Bath Club. When she was thirteen, she was allowed to accept the presidency of the Children's League of the Princess Elizabeth of York Hospital, which had been named after her.

There remained the question, both practical and philosophical, of what an Heiress Presumptive and future Queen should be educated to be like – a conundrum that had not faced the Court or Government since the 1830s, when Princess Victoria's education had been entrusted to the remarkable Baroness Lehzen. Marion Crawford had been employed to help the princesses become lady-like, not monarchical. After George VI's accession, there was a hesitant appreciation that being lady-like was not enough, but there remained a tension between the training felt suitable for a Head of State, and the needs of an idealized princess. The result was an incongruous mix. If the notion, as an authorized account claimed, that the Princess was subjected to 'a strenuous tutelage increasing in measure with the passing years',[47] was simply a pious invention, there was at least some expansion of the curriculum. Princess Elizabeth began to take twice weekly lessons in constitutional history at Eton College, close to Windsor Castle and Royal Lodge, given by the Vice-Provost, Henry (later Sir Henry) Marten. Later this tuition was supplemented by that of the Vicomtesse de Bellaigue, who taught both princesses French, French literature and European history.[48] Yet there was also a deep concern to avoid the taint of an 'intellectual' as opposed to 'practical' princess. It was therefore announced that she was taking cooking lessons in the Royal Lodge kitchens, that she sometimes baked cakes in her little Welsh cottage which were sent to children in hospitals or to unemployed areas, that she had learnt to sweep and scrub and to polish furniture, and that Queen Mary, 'a keen housewife,' had admired her efforts.[49]

Marten did his best. The theme of his tutelage combined the traditional and the modern, reminding the Princess of where she came from, but also of the changes wrought by modern conditions. Later, he recalled teaching her that the British Monarchy was exceeded in antiquity only by the papacy, that it went back more than a millennium to King Egbert, 'the first to unite all England,' and that the secret of its survival was its ability to adapt. He also taught her what he considered the two great events affecting the Monarchy in their own time, the 1931 Statute of Westminster and the advent of broadcasting. The Statute, he explained, had founded the modern British Commonwealth by making a common allegiance to the Crown the sole surviving link between Great Britain and the Dominions; while broadcasting enabled the Royal Family, by talking personally on the air, to sustain that link.[50] How much his pupil retained is hard to say, though he may have fired her interest in the past a little. When Princess Marie Louise apologized over dinner at Windsor during the Second World War for indulging in an old lady's reminiscences, the teenage Princess replied: 'But Cousin Louise, it's *history*, and therefore so thrilling.'[51] But perhaps she was just being polite.

Yet if the Princess began to build up an academic knowledge from her tutor, as well as an extraordinary acquaintanceship with some of the major players on the world stage, if she was known to millions of young people all over the world and occasionally seen by a few thousand of them – she nevertheless remained separate from all but a handful of carefully selected contemporaries, with few of whom she could ever be close. There is always a sense of the goldfish bowl, and the lack of any direct contact through the glass.

In some ways, she was very mature for her age. Physically, she developed early, with 'big bosoms just like her mother', as a member of a courtier family, who played kick-the-tin with her at Balmoral in the late 1930s, fondly recalls.[52] In other ways, silk stockings notwithstanding, she was held back in childhood. Marten remembered teaching 'a somewhat shy girl of thirteen who when asked a question would look for confidence and support to her beloved governess, Miss Crawford.'[53] Crawfie herself suggests a lonely, yet self-sufficient, child, and one with her own private world of perplexity. She recalled seeing her stand for hours at the window at Buckingham Palace, looking down the Mall towards Admiralty Arch, and that she would ask her questions 'about the world outside'.[54] The picture of a young princess who lacked nothing except social intercourse with people who did not think of her, first and always, as a princess, is confirmed by Elizabeth's own recollections. When she was having her portrait painted in the Yellow Drawing-Room by Pietro Annigoni shortly after her own Accession, she told the artist that she had spent hours as a child in the same huge, magnificent room, looking out of the windows. 'I loved watching the people and the cars there in the Mall,' she said. 'They all seemed so busy. I used to wonder what they were doing and where they were all going, and what they thought about outside the Palace.'[55]

WAR, AND THE threat of war, ups the value of Monarchy. As the danger from Hitler grew, and the rearmament programme gathered pace, the King and Queen became increasingly busy as hosts, ambassadors and patriotic symbols. Two days before the signing of the Munich agreement in the autumn of 1938, the twelve-year-old Princess Elizabeth travelled with her mother to Clydebank for the launch of the giant Cunard liner *Queen Elizabeth*, destined to be used both for civilian passengers and as a troop ship. Usually, however, the royal couple did their visiting and travelling unaccompanied by their children who, it was felt, were better off at home. In the case of the foreign trips which the King and Queen were now required to make, there was no sense that, quite apart from the advantages of keeping the family together, seeing other countries would be educational.

The most important royal visit of the decade took place in 1939. Following a brief and apparently successful trip to France in July 1938 to strengthen the Entente Cordiale, it was decided to send the royal couple to North America, to strengthen the special relationship. Before the journey, President Roosevelt invited 'either or both' the princesses, genially observing in his letter that 'I shall try to have one or two

Roosevelts of approximately the same age to play with them!' It was an exciting offer, but the King declined it, on the grounds that they were too young for the rigours of the Canadian part of the tour.[56]

By the time of embarkation in May 1939, Franco had taken Madrid, Hitler had marched into Prague, and a full-scale European conflict seemed imminent. Interest in the tour on both sides of the Atlantic was intense. Perhaps the wild excitement that greeted the King and Queen from the moment they landed in Canada on 17 May would have been even greater if their daughters had been with them. As it was, the visitors had to content themselves with the first-ever royal transatlantic telephone call, taken by the princesses at the Bowes-Lyon house at St. Paul's Walden Bury.[57] The King and Queen spoke through hand microphones; the children finished their end of the conversation by holding the Queen's corgi and making him bark by pinching him.[58]

After three weeks in Canada, the King and Queen were fêted in the United States by the President ('He is so easy to get to know,' wrote a grateful Monarch, '& never makes one feel shy'), before re-embarking from Canada on 15 June. Deeply moved by his reception, and relieved that it was over, the King 'nearly cried' – as he later confessed – at the end of his final speech before departing. It was, wrote his biographer, 'a climacture in the King's life,' while at the same time 'an undeniable wrench to leave homeland and family under such uncertain conditions'.[59]

Presumably it was also a wrench for his children, despite the telephone call. In the press, the six-week parting was widely discussed as an example of the high level of sacrifice the royal couple were prepared to make for the public good. Some interest was also taken in the feelings of their daughters, and the leave-taking at Portsmouth at the beginning of the trip became a moment of sentimental drama.

Keen attention was paid to the princesses as they were taken aboard their parents' ship before she sailed. Elizabeth at thirteen, it was observed, was nearly as tall as her mother. There was a change in the way she dressed – no longer in 'babyish, bonnet-shaped hats,' wearing instead a tilted cap, with the hem-line of her coat and dress lowered to below her knees.[60] The faces of both girls were scrutinized for signs of emotion. According to one witness, 'they looked somewhat forlorn when, at length, amid tremendous cheering, the hooting of sirens, and the God-speed of thousands of onlookers, the mighty liner, bearing their Majesties, slowly glided out of the harbour.'[61] According to another, when the princesses returned to the jetty, 'Margaret's face puckered up, Elizabeth looked tearful . . . ,' while the King and Queen could be seen gazing after them, 'until the two little figures merged into the blue of thronged quays'.[62]

During the tour, Elizabeth sent her mother photographs, and made a film of Margaret and the pets with a cine-camera. Various diversions of an educational sort were arranged by Queen Mary. One was a visit to the Bank of England to see the gold in the vaults. Naturally, the Governor, Montagu Norman, accompanied them. The old Queen was sincere in her didactic aims. However, in the prevailing mood such excursions almost inevitably became public events as well as private ones, despite strenuous efforts by Buckingham Palace to prevent, or at any rate contain, publicity. 'I think that the question of the press and press photographers in connection with the outings of T.R.H.s Princess Elizabeth and Princess Margaret will have to be seriously considered,' Sir Eric Miéville, the courtier responsible for press relations, wrote to the King's private secretary following a trip to London Zoo which was widely covered in the picture papers. 'What happens now is that by some extraordinary means, unknown to me, whenever they are due to visit an institution, news always leaks out ahead to certain members of the press . . . One has to remember that in these days such information given to the newspapers is worth money.'[63]

The homecoming of the King and Queen was almost as dramatic as the departure. The princesses prepared for it by spring-cleaning the 'Little House'.[64] The press did so by sending every available reporter to Southampton, where a destroyer, the *Kempenfelt*, had been ordered to carry the children to the liner *Empress of Britain* for a family reunion. 'Blue eyes sparkling, hair blowing,' the girls were piped on board the *Kempenfelt*.[65] Solemnly, they shook hands with each of the ship's officers, before sailing out to meet their parents in the Solent. After they had been brought together and returned to shore, the whole royal party proceeded by train to Waterloo, whence they rode in state to Buckingham Palace, the two princesses beside the King and Queen in the leading carriage.

4

'WE NEVER SEEMED to get really settled again after the Canada-America visit of 1939,' recalled Crawfie.[1] The trip marked the end of the tight family life that had survived the move out of 145 Piccadilly, and the start of intermittent separations and comings-together that lasted until 1945. The Royal Family had a good war – by the standards of almost every other royal house a stupendous one, emerging with its reputation enhanced, and much of the damage done by the Abdication repaired. Yet the psychology of the achievement was complicated. Much depended on the passivity of the Symbol King, and the serenity of his family life. Loyalty to the Monarchy waxed as the nation's fear grew, and acquired a character of hope and yearning – different from the sentimentalities and social conservatism of peacetime – which, as the end approached, turned to gratitude toward a King who had no way of affecting the outcome. Meanwhile, his children became representatives of what the fighting was about, their pre-war immaturity and innocence frozen in aspic. 'One felt,' in the words of a writer of the period, 'that these engaging little people would never grow up'.[2] The symbolism was heightened by a mystery. For security reasons, the whereabouts of the girls were kept secret, and the images of them that appeared in the press were set against an unknown, unidentifiable background, adding to a sense of them as magical princesses whose fate was linked to the national destiny.

The Royal Family was at Balmoral until just before the declaration of war on September 3rd. The King returned to London on August 23rd, his wife five days later. The children were despatched to Birkhall, the first of their mysterious locations, where they were cared for and guarded by a retinue headed by an equerry, and including a chauffeur, a police sergeant and several constables.[3] Lessons of a sort continued, Crawfie reading newspapers out loud, 'trying as far as possible to give them some idea of what was happening without too many horrible details.'[4] Marten posted history papers, and Princess Elizabeth sent him essays for correction. Girl Guide meetings took place in the village hall. So did 'war-work', which consisted of a large sewing party mainly made up of women from the royal estate. At Christmas they went to Sandringham, and then to Royal Lodge until May, with the Queen in residence for much of the time. Here there was more Girl Guiding, with the unusual ingredient of evacuees from the East End, bringing the girls into fleeting contact with urban working-class children.

'Thank you so very much for the books you and Mr Chamberlain sent me for my birthday,' Princess Elizabeth wrote to the Prime Minister's wife on 23 April 1940. 'It was so kind of you and I have always wanted to read them. I hope you are both well and that Mr Chamberlain is not too tired. Thanking you again so much.'[5] Mr Chamberlain was, however, shortly to be relieved of his responsibilities. On 8 May , following the debate on the Norway campaign, he was forced to resign. Two days later, Winston Churchill drove to Buckingham Palace to kiss hands as his successor. On 12 May, as Hitler invaded the Low Countries, the princesses were moved into the great fortress of Windsor Castle, where they were to live for most of the war. 'We went there for a weekend,' as Princess Margaret recalls, 'and we stayed for five years.'[6]

For a while, they slept in the dungeons. Princess Margaret remembers having to run to get to the shelter under Brunswick Tower. Yet she thought of it as a happy time.[7] Her sister felt much the same. She later told Harold Nicolson that she would like to make Windsor her home, rather than Buckingham Palace or Sandringham, since all the happiest memories of her childhood were associated with the Castle and the Park.[8] The girls lived in pampered seclusion, in conditions, as Morrah put it after the war, 'favourable to the quiet business of the schoolroom, though perhaps less for the enlargement of human contacts.'[9] There was a shifting band of soldiers, often Grenadier Guards, for company. With an informality hard to imagine in peacetime, they ate with their governesses and one or two officers in the State Dining Room, where a single light bulb hung from the ceiling in place of a chandelier.[10] At first, the King and Queen stayed at Windsor, commuting to Buckingham Palace. Later, after the worst of the bombing, they returned to London, visiting the Castle only at weekends.[11]

How should the royal children be used in wartime? Some of the best minds in the Ministry of Information addressed the problem with, as usual, contradictory results. On the one hand, it was decided to make much of the princesses' privations at a 'place in the country,' where they bore their loneliness stoically, for the national good. On the other, government propaganda used them as the centre-piece to an image of the perfect family hearth, confidently and comfortably immune to the threats of vulgar dictators. To project such an image, they would be shown, in pictures or prose, relaxing on sofas and rugs, surrounded by proud parents and placid pets. These two, separate, ways of imagining the King's daughters were sometimes combined. Later in the war, when victory was in sight, the second tended to predominate. Initially, when the need for sacrifice was greatest, the emphasis was on the first.

The presentation of the girls as victims of the family-rending impact of war provided the theme of Princess Elizabeth's first broadcast, delivered in October 1940 when she was fourteen-and-a-half, and directed at British children evacuated to North America, though actually intended to influence adult opinion in the United States, and the US Government, as well.

That the broadcast took place at all was a retreat by Buckingham Palace and a sign of how dire the emergency had become. Pre-war requests for Princess Elizabeth to speak on the air had been met by curt refusals. In 1938, the influential owner of the *New York Herald Tribune*, Helen Reid, was brusquely rebuffed when she asked if the Princess might make a five-minute broadcast to open National Children's Week in the United States. Mrs Reid had used the powerful argument that such a gesture would be in keeping with the British Government's policy of doing everything possible to bring America and Great Britain together. She had added, a little less tactfully, that it would also assuage American bitterness over the treatment of the Duke of Windsor at the time of his marriage.[12] Referring the matter to Buckingham Palace, the British ambassador wrote dismissively of such 'attempts to enlist the princesses for stunts'.[13] The Palace strongly agreed, and confirmed 'that there is, of course, no question of the princesses broadcasting, nor is it likely to be considered for many years to come'.[14] The autumn of 1940, however, was no time to be fastidious, where a chance of influencing American public opinion was concerned. When the Director-General of the BBC, Frederick Ogilvie, approached the King's private secretary, he immediately received a favourable answer.

The plan was to get Princess Elizabeth to introduce a series of 'Children in Wartime' programmes, intended to bring out the part children could play in the nation's defence. The Princess's brief statement would go out live in the short-wave service to the United States and Canada, and later be heard in recorded form all over the world. The unofficial aim of pulling adult heartstrings was made clear to the King and Queen. 'As Her Royal Highness's first broadcast, delivered at an historic moment,' Ogilvie explained to the Palace, 'it would reach the minds of the millions who heard it with a singular poignancy.'[15]

The broadcast went out on 13 October. The Princess read a carefully scripted text which linked her own recent life and that of her sister to the lives of displaced British children overseas. 'Thousands of you in this country have had to leave your homes and be separated from your father and mother,' she told her listeners, in a high-pitched, precise voice which *The Times* likened to that of her mother.[16] 'My sister Margaret Rose and I feel so much for you, as we know from experience what it means to be away from those we love most of all.' There was an expression of optimism ('We know, every one of us, that in the end all will be well.') A final exchange with the ten-year-old Princess Margaret was also in the prepared text: 'My sister is by my side, and we are both going to say good night to you. Come on, Margaret.' 'Good night,' said a smaller voice. 'Good night and good luck to you all.'[17]

Jock Colville, private secretary to the Prime Minister and later to Princess Elizabeth, wrote in his diary that he and Diana Sandys, Winston Churchill's daughter, who listened to the broadcast with him, 'were embarrassed by the sloppy sentiment she was made to express, but her voice was most impressive and, if the Monarchy survives, Queen Elizabeth II should be a most successful radio Queen'.[18] Sloppiness was what the occasion seemed to require: the broadcast was hailed on both sides of the Atlantic as a propaganda triumph, at a time when triumphs of any kind were sparse. It attracted particularly wide attention in the United States and made the front pages, with a picture in all the New York papers. 'Princess yesterday huge success here,' the local BBC representative cabled to Ogilvie. 'Some stations report telephone exchanges jammed with requests for repeat.'[19] Such was the quantity and enthusiasm of fan mail that the BBC turned the broadcast into a gramophone record for sale in America and throughout the Empire.

The guise of the princesses as typically lonely displaced children reinforced another part of the Ministry of Information's offensive: a projection of the King and Queen as typical Londoners carrying on regardless in spite of the Blitz. It helped to give the broadcast impact, indeed it might almost have been part of the plot, that Buckingham Palace had received a direct hit a few weeks earlier. Pictures of brave little girls in the country and their brave parents among the rubble mixed together in the public imagination. Mass Observation, the precursor of in-depth polling, recorded a mood of indignation and defiance, in which royalty played a part. 'If they hurt the King and Queen or the princesses we'd be so mad we'd blast every German out of existence,' declared a supposedly typical female clerk.[20]

Sometimes the children were shown on a pony cart with a corgi beside them, without adults, alone in a park. According to one early wartime account, walkers near their home would 'meet the two girls jogging along hatless, laughing, and talking merrily, taking it in turns to hold the reins, which they do gracefully with ribbons threaded in orthodox fashion over the first finger and under the thumb of the left hand'.[21] The impression was of free spirits, self-sufficient and unharmed in their own secret world. The contrast between this fairy land and bombed-out cities was stark. But there was also the other guise: children in the perfect family, whose domestic happiness was to be protected by the soldiers, sailors and airmen of the Empire as if it were their own. In this version, the children were never alone. Indeed, the presence of the King and Queen was a key ingredient.

It was important, as Simon Schama has observed, that a monarchy should appear as 'the family of families, at once dynastic and domestic, remote and accessible, magical and mundane'.[22] In a total war, the importance of the Windsors' as the 'family of families' increased because conditions on the home front, in addition to the foreign danger, were shaking non-royal family life to its foundations. The same had been true in the First World War. However, there had been a significant shift since 1914–18, partly because of the milder temperament of George VI, compared to his father, and the circumstances of his accession; and partly because his Royal Family, unlike the one he was born into, was conveniently young, nuclear and comprehensible. In the First War, George V had been portrayed as patriarchal, even god-like, a warrior monarch to whom duty was owed. In the Second World War, the whole 'family of families' was given prominence as a unit, with the King and Queen frequently shown in the company of their children, underscoring the domestic affections and virtues that the war was about.

Here it is particularly difficult to separate image from reality, because witnesses to royal domesticity were subject to the same media messages as everybody else, and the dutiful Windsors themselves, hounded by the pressures of what was expected of them, were on their best behaviour when being observed. In the context of such necessary and powerful myths, the royal actors had little choice but to play their allotted parts.

Would Edward VIII, had he lasted, have been selfish and truculent in wartime, or would he have risen to the occasion? It is an interesting speculation. As it was, the stammering King whom some had believed could not survive the ordeal of being crowned, seemed able to adapt in war, as in peace, to the requirements of his job. These consisted mainly of being photographed, taking part in public ceremonies, and personally bestowing honours – sometimes, because of the fighting, decorating several hundred servicemen in a single session. It also involved, and this was an especially vital role, making important visitors feel pleased to have had the opportunity of meeting him and his family. Surprisingly, this became something that George VI was particularly good at. The strange combination of his own social ineptitude, the Queen's ability to make whoever she addressed feel that they were the one person to whom she wished to speak, and their daughters' lack of affectation, provided a recipe for putting people at their ease.

Were they as genuinely pleased to see an endless flow of visitors as they seemed, or was it all act? Noël Coward asked himself this question after experiencing what he called 'an exhibition of unqualified "nice-ness" from all concerned' during a meeting with the Royal Family in 1942. He concluded that it did not matter. Putting oneself out was part of the job of royalty. 'I'll settle for anyone who does their job well, anyhow.'[23] Few others, however, came away feeling that it was just for show. For most who encountered the Family informally, the wonder of being in the presence of Monarchy in an Empire at war was combined with an uplifting sense of inclusion, as if they them-selves were family members. The result was a miasma of shared affec-tion, of which the grateful visitor felt both spectator and part. When Queen Alexandra of Yugoslavia (herself a refugee) met them in 1944, she immediately decided that 'this was the sort of home life I wanted, with children and dogs playing at my feet.'[24] General Sir Alan Brooke, Chief of the Imperial General Staff, who spent a shooting weekend with them in Norfolk in the same year, came away with a similar feeling – recording his impression of 'one of the very best examples of family life. A thoroughly close-knit and happy family all wrapped up in each other.'[25]

Nobody referred, in their descriptions of the King, to his intellectual capacities, his political judgement, or his knowledge of the war. Yet so far from being a handicap, George VI's limitations – and his aware-ness of them – were turned into a precious source of strength. One Gentleman Usher fondly described him as 'a plodder' – a man of simple ideas, with a strong sense of what he ought to do. Much was made of such decent ordinariness, which meant confronting what others had to face without complaint – and included such self-denials as not seeking to escape the Blitz, or trying to give his daughters a privileged immunity from danger by sending them with other rich children to Canada. It also meant frugality, and strict obedience to government rules – a topic which played a major part in the use of royalty for propaganda. Thus, in April 1940, the public was informed that at the celebration of Princess Elizabeth's fourteenth birthday, the Queen had decreed that the three-tier anniversary cake should be limited to plain sponge, as an economy.[26] There were many tales of economy with clothing coupons, and of how the Queen cut down and altered her own dresses for Elizabeth, adapting these in turn for Margaret, so that 'with the three of us, we manage in relays'.[27] This was not just for public consumption. When Eleanor Roosevelt visited Buckingham Palace late in 1942, she found an adherence to heat, water and food restrictions that was almost a fetish. Broken window panes in her bedroom had been replaced with wood, and her bath had a painted black line above which she was not supposed to run the water.[28]

Nevertheless, there remained a wide gulf between the life lived by the Royal Family, with their houses, parks and horses, and retinue of servants, and the conditions of their subjects. After a bomb struck the Palace, the Queen was supposed to have said: 'Now we can look the East End in the face'. The East End, however, was not able to retreat to Windsor to catch up on sleep, or to spend recuperative holidays in Norfolk and Scotland. Nor was the East End able to supplement its diet with pheasants and venison shot on the royal estates.

Indeed some aspects of royal life went on remarkably undisturbed. There was little interruption to the riding lessons given to the princesses by Horace Smith, which continued throughout the war. Training with Smith involved pony carts, which (as he later observed) had the particular advantage in wartime that journeys in them did not require petrol. With future troop-reviewing in mind, Smith also taught Princess Elizabeth to ride side-saddle. Occasions for demonstrating equestrian prowess did not cease, either. In 1943, Smith personally awarded Princess Elizabeth first prize in the Royal Windsor Horse Show for her driving of a 'utility vehicle,' harnessed to her own black Fell pony – a trophy she won again the following year, both times in the presence of the King and Queen.[29]

Watching was a developing interest, as well as riding or driving. In the spring of 1942, the Princess was taken by her parents to the Beckhampton stables on the Wiltshire Downs, where horses bred at the royal studs were trained, to see two royal horses, Big Game and Sun Chariot, which were highly fancied for the Derby and the Oaks. The jockey Sir Gordon Richards later recalled his meeting with the sixteen-year-old girl 'who took them all in', and was quizzed about them by her father as they worked, causing the royal trainer Fred Darling to remark loyally 'that Princess Elizabeth must have a natural eye for a horse'. Visits to see the mares and foals at the royal stud at

Hampton Court, and to see the royal horses in training at Newmarket followed.[30]

Other pursuits also involved opportunities not available to most compatriots. In October 1942, Princess Elizabeth made her contribution to the royal larder by shooting her first stag in the hills at Balmoral – using a rifle she had been taught to handle the previous year.[31] In the autumn of 1943, she hunted with the Garth Foxhounds, and later with the Duke of Beaufort's Hounds in Gloucestershire.[32] The decision to allow her to go hunting was taken, according to a report, 'in accord with the general policy of making her life as "normal" as possible' in the light of her position as Heiress Presumptive.[33]

There were also private entertainments. The King, despite his shyness, was a good dancer, and especially enjoyed dancing in the company of his children. He did not allow the war to curtail this particular pastime. A number of royal balls were held. Princess Elizabeth attended her first at Windsor in July 1941, when she was fifteen. A West End dance band played foxtrots, waltzes and rumbas to the Royal Family and their guests, who included Guards officers, until two in the morning, and Elizabeth danced several times with her father.[34] Later in the war, before the start of flying bombs in 1944, dances were held fortnightly in the Bow Room on the ground floor at Buckingham Palace. On one occasion the King, oblivious to cares of state, his stammer forgotten, led his family and other guests in a conga line through the corridors and state rooms.[35]

FOR MAXIMUM BENEFIT to the war effort, the privacy of the Royal Family needed to be less than complete. If life at Windsor and Buckingham Palace had been simply private, its exemplary virtues could scarcely have been known to loyal subjects. For this reason, as The Times observed just after the end of the war, 'many glimpses' of the Royal Family's home life had 'reached a wide public, through illustrated journals and the cinema'.[36] One avid supplier to the illustrated journals, and propagator of royal mythology, was the photographer Lisa Sheridan who, by her own testimony, never failed to come away from a professional visit to the Royal Family without feeling a better person. Her recollections of the princesses in wartime are interesting not only because her pictures of wagging puppy tails, happy children and proud parents became fixed in the Empire's imagination, but also because she provides a distillation of the 'family of families' miasma in its purest form.

In her memoirs, Mrs Sheridan described several wartime trips to see the princesses. Her account of the first, to Royal Lodge in early 1940, reflected the official line of the phoney war period, that the enemy had done little to change the traditional British way of life. The windows 'showed no signs of criss-cross sticky tape or nasty black-out'. The princesses were intent on their normal recreations. When she arrived, they were dressed for riding and carried crops; they changed into 'sensible' tweed skirts and pullovers, in order to be photographed in the garden, suitably equipped with rakes and barrows, digging for victory. The overriding impression, however, was of the Windsors as a household anyone would like to be part of. Apart from the King and Queen and a policeman at the gate, nobody else was visible. 'I never felt the presence of anyone at all other than the family,' she recalled. It was clear 'that home was to the Royal Family the source of life itself and that there was a determination on the part of the King and Queen to maintain a simple, united family life, whatever calls there might be to duty'. Later visits reinforced this picture of self-containment, though the background shifted from the unchanging domesticity of Royal Lodge to the warlike ramparts of the Castle. Here there were parables of life and death: the demise of a pet chameleon, for example ('Princess Elizabeth could not bring herself to speak of her tiny pet for quite a long time after his death') and, even more painfully, the death of a favourite corgi. The Queen, however, as always comforting and wise, told her elder daughter to keep things in proportion. It was, after all, the height of a world war.[37]

Sheridan's photographs, disseminated among dusty desert rats, weary Bevin boys, homesick land girls and traumatized evacuees, show a precious, sheltered intactness. In Sheridan's world, the princesses were happily free from the requirement to do anything except obligingly change their outfits, and display an exquisite politeness. Yet they were also shown to be greatly concerned about the worrying state of a world mercifully beyond their comprehension – a concern that helpfully linked the 'perfect hearth' portrayal of the photographic image to a view of the girls which provided the regular diet of Ministry of Information handouts: as dutiful models for every other daughter of the Empire too young to serve in the women's services.

A series of newspaper reports involving Princess Elizabeth, in particular, were designed, not so much to idealize the Heiress Presumptive, as to indicate royal approval for Government-sponsored schemes. Thus, the princesses did not only dig for victory, they knitted for it – the product of their labours being divided, with judicious impartiality, between the men of the army, navy and air force.[38] When they ran out of materials, there was a solution: in July 1941 it was announced that the two girls, aged fifteen and eleven, had personally arranged, and performed in, a concert in front of their parents and members of the armed services, from which between £70 and £80 had been raised, 'to buy wool for knitting for the Forces'. If a Ministry wished to exhort the population to greater efforts, or advertise an achievement, it turned to the Palace for help, and where appropriate, royal children were provided. On one occasion the princesses (to the envy of every school child) were shown over a Fortress bomber, and allowed to play with the controls. On another, orchestrated publicity was given to the Queen's decision to have both of them immunized against diphtheria. On yet another, the Heiress Presumptive was designated by the Ministry of Works as the donor of a prize open to Welsh schoolchildren 'for the best essay in English and Welsh on metal salvage.'[39] Meanwhile, there was a press story in 1941 about how the fifteen-year-old Princess (despite a Civil List income of £6,000 a year) was only allowed five shillings a week pocket money; and that more than half even of this small sum was generously donated to war-supporting good causes.[40] The same spring, royal dolls owned by the children were exhibited to raise money for the British War Relief Society,[41] and a special 'Princess Elizabeth's Day' was announced, for collecting for children's charities.

How could any teenager cope? One answer is that royalty lived its life in compartments: the public sectioned off from the private and, in the case of a young princess, often barely touching her personally at all. Another is that teenagers had not yet been invented – or at any rate, young people in their teens in the early 1940s had very different expectations from those either before or after the war. The Second World War was a time when adolescence was held in suspension. Children who went straight from school into war work or the armed services, enjoyed no intervening period of irresponsibility. In this, Princess Elizabeth was not unusual. The acceptance of a variety of honorific titles or the performance of symbolic acts was not necessarily more stressful than the tasks and ways of life of many contemporaries. Nevertheless, at a stage in life when it is hard enough to keep everyday private events in perspective, such a cacophony of public roles provided a strange accompaniment to growing up.

She was like other girls of her age, yet not like them. Winston Churchill was supposed to have remarked in an unflattering reference to Clement Attlee, that if you feed a grub on royal jelly, it becomes a queen. In the case of a human Heiress Presumptive, the equivalent of royal jelly is the world's perceptions: the drip feed of curtseys, deference, public recognition, combined with a knowledge of lack of choice, and of inevitability. The strongest instinct of many adolescents is to conform: it was an instinct with which Princess Elizabeth was well equipped. She seems to have dealt with the peculiarity of her position by becoming as unremarkable as possible in everything she could not change, while accepting absolutely what was expected of her. Her actual experience was unique: there was nobody with whom she could compare herself, no peer group to set a standard. Yet few young people could have been more conformist, more amenable, than George VI's elder daughter.

There remains the difficulty for the rest of humanity – grubs without a destiny – in understanding the mentality of somebody with such extraordinary expectations. A distinctive character, however, was beginning to emerge. Authentic portraits are rare – *vignettes* by passing visitors are generally coloured by excitement at meeting royalty, and tell more about the witness than the subject. But there are enough thoughtful descriptions to confirm the part-flattering, part-disconcerting impressions provided by Crawfie, of a reserved, strong-willed, narrow-visioned, slightly priggish child, without intellectual or aesthetic interests, taking what she is given as part of the natural order, but with greater mental capacities than any close member of the family cared to appreciate. When she was still thirteen, the Archbishop of Canterbury, Cosmo Lang, noted after 'a full talk with the little lady alone' before he conducted her confirmation service, that 'though naturally not very communicative, she showed real intelligence and understanding'.[42] More than two years later, Eleanor Roosevelt formed a view of her that was strikingly similar. The wife of one Head of State assessed the daughter of another as 'quite serious and a child with a great deal of character and personality ... She asked me a number of questions about life in the United States and they were serious questions.'[43]

The experience of her as an able, but above all single-minded, young person was shared by Horace Smith, who had more contact with her during the war than any of her other teachers apart from Crawfie, and who taught her in the subject that interested her most. The Princess was not, he considered, 'a person who takes up interests lightly, only to drop them just as easily a short time later. If and when her interest is aroused, she goes into whatever subject it is with thoroughness and application, nor does her interest wane with the passing of time or the claim of other new matters upon her attention.' In addition, he noted, she had 'a keen and retentive mind'.[44]

Such perceptions were combined, however, with a sense that she was young for her age, and remained in appearance and manner still a child until well into her teens. Perhaps there was an element of wishful thinking: the princesses' childhood was part of the *status quo ante bellum* which it was hoped to restore. Such a feeling may have been strongest of all in the King and Queen, who liked her to wear the clothes of a child after she had ceased to be one. Nevertheless an uncertainty about whether Princess Elizabeth was precocious or immature, or both, is a recurrent feature of the accounts. Chips Channon observed the princesses in procession at a service at St. Paul's in May 1943, 'dressed alike in blue, which made them seem like little girls'.[45] Peter Townsend, an RAF officer who joined the Royal Family as an equerry to the King nine months later, found that they were not too old to lead him in a 'hair-raising bicycle race,' and recalled Princess Elizabeth as 'charming and totally unsophisticated'.[46] Alexandra of Yugoslavia's recollection of meeting her British cousins at Windsor, describes a childish ritual involving the princesses and their dogs. When tea was brought in, they insisted on feeding (with the aid of a footman) their four corgis first.[47]

Preparation for her osmosis from child-princess, locked in a tower with her schoolbooks or playing in the park with her sister, to constitutionally responsible Heiress, was scratchy, like much else in wartime. For some time, the Crawfie and Marten regime had been supplemented with French lessons from the Vicomtesse de Bellaigue. According to one of the Queen's ladies-in-waiting, Lady Helen Graham, Elizabeth had been encouraged to attend closely to the news bulletins of the BBC.[48] 'Already the Princess has a first-rate knowledge of State and current affairs,' a courtier declared in 1943.[49]

Various accounts were given of the level of her knowledge, some of them doubtless exaggerated, in order to demonstrate her fitness for the tasks ahead. It was said that, in addition to French, she was fluent in German. When she was eighteen, *The Times* claimed she was highly musical and although 'like some others of her sex, she is no mathematician,' she was familiar with 'many classics' in English and French.[50] When a magazine editor wrote to the Palace to check a list, supplied by 'a friend near the Court,' of books and authors the Princess had allegedly read, a courtier replied firmly that the list could be published as correct. It consisted of 'many of Shakespeare's plays,' Chaucer's *Canterbury Tales*, Coleridge, Keats, Browning, Tennyson, Scott, Dickens, Austen, Trollope, Stevenson, Trevelyan's *History of England*, Conan Doyle, Buchan and Peter Cheyney.[51] To this remarkably large collection might be added the Brontës: at the end of the war, Lisa Sheridan found the Princess reading *Jane Eyre* and *Wuthering Heights*, and expressing a preference for historical novels and stories about the Highlands.[52] Was it true? If such accounts were even half accurate, the Princess would have been a strong candidate for a place at university, where she might have extended her intellectual range. Neither university nor even finishing school, however, was considered as a possibility. Instead, like a butcher or a joiner, she apprenticed for the job she would be undertaking for the rest of her life by doing it.

Her first practical experience of the grown-up world of royalty was to head a regiment. In January 1942, following the death of the Duke of Connaught, she was asked to take his place as honorary Colonel of the Grenadier Guards – a natural choice, some felt, in view of her contact with the Grenadiers at Windsor. The offer was accepted, and on her sixteenth birthday she carried out her first engagement as Colonel at Windsor Castle, inspecting the Grenadiers in the company of her father. Thirty reporters and ten photographers were granted press passes to cover the event.[53] Cecil Beaton marked it with one of his most famous pictures, which shows the Heiress Presumptive in uniform, fresh-faced and half-smiling, with her jacket unbuttoned and her hat at a coquettish angle. Afterwards, she was hostess to more than six hundred officers and men, entertained by the comedian Tommy Handley.[54] The Grenadier Guards were delighted by their acquisition, and those who dined with her in the officers' mess recall her as 'charming, and very sincere'.[55] Yet despite this dramatic début, Buckingham Palace kept up the fiction that the Princess was still a child, and American press requests for help with a story about her were met with the incomprehensible denial that she was entering public life.[56]

Adulthood could not be postponed for ever. Princess Elizabeth's coming-of-age, when she was entitled to succeed to the throne without need for a Regent, took place when she was eighteen, in April 1944. There was no débutante ball to celebrate the occasion. Instead, it was accompanied by the Princess's graduation from a nursery bedroom to a suite. Here she was pictured by Lisa Sheridan, as if she were part of the interior design. 'The upholstery is pale pink brocade patterned in cream,' it was revealed. 'The walls are cream, hung with peaceful pictures of pastoral scenes. The Princess's flowered frock harmonized admirably with her room.'[57] There were other changes, to mark her rise in status. She was assigned her own armorial bearings, and her own standard which flew in whatever residence she happened to be occupying. She also acquired a 'Household' of her own, including, in July 1944, a lady-in-waiting. Meanwhile, she had unwittingly stimulated a minor constitutional controversy which engaged the best legal brains for several months.

The 1937 Regency Act, which had been passed following George VI's accession, had provided for two forms of delegation of royal powers: to a Regent, in the event of a child under eighteen succeeding, or of the total incapacitation of a monarch; and to five Counsellors of State, composed of the Consort and the four next in line of succession, in the event of the Sovereign's illness or absence abroad. However, the provision disqualified anybody not 'a British subject of full age,' which effectively meant that Elizabeth could succeed her father as Queen with full powers at eighteen, but not deputise for him as a Counsellor until she was twenty-one.[58]

Nobody noticed this anomaly until an eagle-eyed lawyer pointed it out to the King's private secretary, Sir Alexander Hardinge, in the autumn of 1942. Hardinge at first dismissed it. It was 'common sense,' he replied to the lawyer tartly, to regard the Princess as fully of age if she could succeed without a Regent.[59] The Lord Chancellor, Lord Simon, however, disagreed: due to bad drafting, the law and common sense did not coincide.[60] There the matter might have rested, had not the King himself indicated his desire to have his daughter as a Counsellor of State. The Lord Chancellor was once again consulted, and recommended to the Prime Minister that the law be changed in order to permit the Heiress Presumptive to become a Counsellor, bearing in mind 'the qualities of the young lady and the wish of her parents'.[61] As Allied troops invaded Sicily in July 1943, George VI spoke to Winston Churchill on the matter, and secured a promise that it should be brought up at War Cabinet, with a view to a quick Bill. 'He quite agrees this should be done,' wrote the King.[62] Cabinet assented, and in October, the Labour Home Secretary in the wartime Coalition, Herbert Morrison, introduced legislation, arguing that the responsibility would give the Heiress valuable experience.

The new Act received the Royal Assent in time for the eighteen-year-old Princess to become a Counsellor, along with her mother and three others, during her father's visit to Italy in July 1944. In his absence she performed her first constitutional functions, which included signifying the Royal Assent to Acts which had been passed by Parliament. Yet she was still not 'a British subject of full age', or legally old enough to vote in an election.

A further question also arose in connection with the Princess's eighteenth birthday: the possibility of a change of title. During 1943, letters and articles appeared in the press suggesting that, in view of her unchallenged position as Heiress, it would be appropriate to designate her 'Princess of Wales,' an idea first mooted in 1936. In August, Pwllheli Town Council petitioned the Prime Minister on the subject,[63] recommending the Princess's birthday as a suitable moment. At the end of the year, the *Carmarthen Journal* reported that no project in recent years had been more popular,[64] and early in 1944, the Welsh

Parliamentary Party, composed of Conservative, Liberal and Labour MPs, joined the campaign. It was pointed out, on all sides, that such a gesture would be greeted with enthusiasm in the Principality, with great benefits to Anglo-Welsh relations.

The Palace, however, demurred. While appreciating the sentiment behind such a proposal, it was unwilling to be swept along by a wave of populist fervour. The key issue, it decided, was the precedent for such a bestowal of title, and the lack of one. The title 'Prince of Wales' had only ever been given to the Heir Apparent. Princess Elizabeth was merely Heir or Heiress Presumptive. Could the Princess perhaps be promoted from Presumptive to Apparent? The Home Office was asked to investigate. 'I have looked into your question about HRH Princess Elizabeth', J. A. R. Pimlott, a Home Office official, wrote to Sir Eric Miéville. 'Where the heir to the throne is a woman her right of succession is defeasible at any time by the birth of a son to the reigning Sovereign. HRH Princess Elizabeth therefore remains Heir Presumptive till she in fact succeeds.' This had been true, he pointed out, of Victoria in 1837. Though Queen Adelaide, widow of William IV, had no child for seventeen years, it was thought constitutionally advisable in proclaiming the accession of Queen Victoria to guard against the possibility of a posthumous birth. The new Sovereign was therefore proclaimed Queen 'saving the rights of any issue of his Late Majesty King William IV which may be born of His Late Majesty's Consort'.[65]

This, however, was not the end of the matter. Though it dealt with the Presumptive-Apparent problem – by definition, no female could be Apparent – it did not dispose of the issue of whether there was any precedent for calling a female Heir, even though only Presumptive, by the Welsh title. Indeed, an inquiry seemed to show, on the basis of records kept by a sixteenth-century German ambassador, that Henry VIII had considered that whichever of his daughters was Heir to the throne should be known as Princess of Wales.[66] For a short time, there was consternation, and uncertainty. However, the evidence to support such a claim was shadowy, and when it was put to Sir Gerald Wollaston, Garter Principal King of Arms, he was dismissive. He also pointed out the danger of setting a new precedent, opening the doors to the alarming future possibility, if George VI had a son who then married, of there being two Princesses of Wales.[67]

The Palace view hardened. There remained, of course, the political complication of public opinion, which would be disappointed, especially in Wales, by a negative decision. But the King's new private secretary, Sir Alan Lascelles, regarded this as a minor factor. 'I have no doubt that the matter will be raised in Parliament before long, and of course the Commons have a right to do so,' he wrote to the King in January 1944, shortly before the Allied forces landed in Anzio. 'As long ago as 1376, they petitioned Edward III to make his grandson, Richard of Bordeaux, Prince of Wales.'[68] Not everybody, however, agreed that the views of parliamentarians should be as readily ignored in the twentieth century as in the fourteenth. One objector was Herbert Morrison, who suggested that to make the King's elder daughter Princess of Wales would deal neatly with any suggestion that the Government was anti-Welsh. It did not matter, Morrison reasonably suggested, if there was no precedent. Moreover, in the unlikely event of a male heir being born, the title could simply lapse.

The Home Secretary's minute on the subject of 28th January 1944 was sent to the Palace, but Lascelles, no mean politician on issues he regarded as important, deliberately withheld it from the King.[69] Probably it made no difference. A few days earlier, Jock Colville recorded in his diary that, while the Cabinet approved of the idea of making Elizabeth Princess of Wales, her father did not.[70] The royal will prevailed. At his weekly audience, Churchill promised the King that he would tell the Minister of Information to 'damp down all discussion of this question in the Press,' in order to avoid a row. In February, it was officially announced from Buckingham Palace that there would be no change in the Princess's title on her eighteenth birthday. 'This will check the spate of press comment and general chatter,' Lascelles recorded on 13 February. As a result, the principality was without a Prince or Princess until 1958. The oft-repeated explanation for this vacancy was 'the very real distinction between heirs apparent and presumptive'.[71]

To CONSOLE the Welsh, the King and Queen took Princess Elizabeth with them on a tour of mining and industrial areas in South Wales early in 1944. The crowds were welcoming and forgiving, and came from all classes and occupations. At Cardiff docks, according to one report, the Queen and Princess 'mingled with a crowd of coloured Merchant Navy seamen,' and stood beside 'an ebony giant from British Honduras'. People from the villages walked for several miles just to see the King's daughter, who smiled and bowed her head in acknowledgement of greetings.[72]

It was not just in Wales, however, that there was an upsurge of feeling in favour of Elizabeth. As the war entered its final phase, she found herself an emblematic heroine everywhere. All over the Empire, the health, beauty and emerging womanhood of the Princess were linked to the eagerly anticipated future, in which families would be brought together, sweethearts rejoined, babies born, bellies filled and freedom enjoyed. Encouraged by broadcasters and newsreels, young people took a special interest in her. On the Welsh tour, she caused particular excitement among children. In Valletta, on the island of Malta, a thousand school children assembled a few weeks before the Normandy landings to see and cheer a special film depicting scenes from her life.[73]

Requests for public appearances by the Princess now became frequent. For the time being the Palace was adamant: there could be no question of 'independent engagements,' though she might occasionally accompany her parents, as to South Wales.[74] Soon, however, this rule was relaxed. On 23 May 1944, Princess Elizabeth spoke publicly for the first time at the annual meeting of the Queen Elizabeth Hospital for Children in Hackney. In the autumn, she accepted an invitation to launch *HMS Vanguard*, the largest battleship ever built in the British Isles. The ceremony, in Clyde shipyards, was followed by a luncheon at which she read a short speech. The First Lord of the Admiralty, A. V. Alexander, wrote to Lascelles afterwards describing 'the clear and decisive way' in which she carried out both duties.[75]

There remained the question of whether she would enter one of the women's services, and if so, which. Early in 1945, it was decided that she would join the Auxiliary Territorial Service. It was not the obvious choice. In view of her family's naval traditions, the WRNS would have been more natural. The King and Queen were apparently reluctant: there is no reason to doubt Crawfie's account of an eager and determined young woman wearing down the resistance of her parents.[76] At the end of February she was registered as No. 230873 Second Subaltern Elizabeth Alexandra Mary Windsor. The rank was an honorary one, but the training in driving and vehicle-maintenance she underwent at No. 1 Mechanical Transport Training Centre at Aldershot, was genuine. She enjoyed this sole, brief experience of communal education. Several decades later, she told the Labour politician Barbara Castle that it was the only time in her life when she had been able seriously to test her own capabilities against those of others of her age.[77] After six weeks she qualified as a driver, and at the end of July, a few days before the final end to the war, she was promoted to Junior Commander.

'The Princess is to be treated in exactly the same way as any other officer learning at the driving training centre,' maintained the official report at the outset.[78] To back this up, the Queen requested that photographers should not be given any facilities.[79] This, however, did not deter the press, and during her short stay at the Centre she was photographed more intensively than at any time since the Coronation. As a result, she was scarcely just one of the girls. If it was not quite true, as a 1957 assessment put it, that 'the rule of seclusion was maintained and she did not mix with her fellows on the course,'[80] the extent of mucking in, on equal terms, was limited. She kept to the routine of the ATS mess, took her share of duties, and acquired the basics of driving, car mechanics and maintenance. But she returned to Windsor every night to sleep. She also became an unwitting mannequin for the uniform of the service – pictures of her with a spanner, at the wheel of a lorry, leaning on a bonnet, or peering purposefully and fetchingly under one, appeared in the newspapers and magazines of every Allied nation.

In such matters, it was always impossible to disentangle a private motive from the public effort. Since the enrolment of a royal princess could not be kept secret, her participation in the ATS inevitably became part of the morale-boosting display of the Monarchy. It was a similar story with other initiatives that started spontaneously. A particularly striking and, in its way, sad example of the way Royal Family behaviour spilled over from the personal to the public, so that domestic events were turned into courtly contrivance, was provided by a series of Christmas shows put on during the war by Windsor children, with the aid of adult mentors, and performed in front of parents and other members of the Castle community.

These began modestly in 1940 with a simple play, 'The Christmas Child,' in St. George's Hall, with Elizabeth playing one of the three kings, flanked by two boy evacuees. The occasion was enjoyed by everybody, and the princesses, who had been on stage since birth without knowing it, discovered an interest in, and even a talent for, amateur theatricals. The following Christmas, the stakes were raised slightly, and a pantomime, 'Cinderella,' was written for them by a local schoolmaster. Again it was a success, and once again there was a good deal of democratic sharing of tasks and banter in the preparations and rehearsals. The next year, they put on 'Sleeping Beauty,' and Lisa Sheridan described how Princess Elizabeth 'took the arms of the two "sailors" and sang "Mind Your Sisters"' and brought the house down.[81] The tradition continued, giving pleasure to both performers and audience, which always included the princesses' parents. Horace Smith, who attended the pantomimes of 1942–4, recalled seeing the elder princess 'full of confidence and vigour,' and reducing the King to hearty laughter.[82] The humour depended a lot on puns. 'There are three acres in one rood,' Widow Twankey, an office boy from the Castle, was required to say in the 1943 production of 'Aladdin'. 'We don't want anything improper,' replied Margaret. 'There's a large copper in the kitchen,' said the Widow. 'We'll soon get rid of him,' declared Elizabeth – and so on.[83]

Year by year, the performances became more polished, with increasingly elaborate costumes and sets. It was also established, as Court etiquette apparently required, that if the King and Queen were to attend, their daughters should have leading parts, regardless of the acting ability of the evacuees and village children who were also involved. Consequently, attention focused on the royal children and their skills, even more than would have been true in any case. Meanwhile audiences grew, bringing in large numbers of locally-based guardsmen and ATS girls. In 1943, there were three performances, including one specifically for soldiers. The show also became publicly known. Weeks before the 1943 pantomime, advance publicity produced a flood of inquiries, and more than a thousand would-be ticket holders sent in applications containing blank cheques. All were politely refused.[84] However, those denied entry could still learn about the show second-hand, for reports appeared in the press. Particular interest was aroused by 'Aladdin' in 1943, in which the Heiress Presumptive, cast in the title role, and wearing utility shorts and top, performed a tap dance, and in one scene appeared as a charlady, in an apron of sackcloth. 'From the moment Princess Elizabeth popped out of a laundry basket,' enthused the *Sunday Graphic*, 'the King and Queen and the audience of 400 laughed and thoroughly enjoyed the show.'[85] After seeing the last of the three performances, Lascelles wrote in his diary that the principals and chorus alike would not have disgraced Drury Lane. 'P'cess Eliz. was a charming Aladdin', he noted, 'and P'cess M. a charming and competent Princess Roxana'.[86] Altogether the pantomime netted £200.

The final pantomime, at Christmas 1944, starred the Heiress Presumptive as a Victorian seaside belle. It also included a carefully choreographed 'ballet interlude,' arranged by the dancing mistress at Buckingham Palace.[87] By this time, however, it had been transformed into an ambitious, semi-professional extravaganza, widely discussed as an established rite, and, in effect, part of the public relations of royalty.

5

BEING ON STAGE was, of course, an inescapable part of a royal
childhood. Indeed, the last of the Windsor shows was followed
by a royal performance as theatrical as anything the princesses had
yet experienced. In contrast to the run-up to the 1918 Armistice which
was brought about by a sudden German collapse, the early months
of 1945 provided a crescendo of victories and liberations. At home,
faith in the cause, pride at survival, and the justice of the outcome,
created a patriotic mood quite different from the nationalist frenzy
of twenty-seven years before. As a result the celebrations marking the
defeat first of Germany and then of Japan contained a communal
spirit which expressed itself in the festival nature of the rejoicing, and
also in an inclusive and grateful attitude to the Royal Family. On both
VE and VJ-Days it was the crowds, as much as the Government, that
placed the King, Queen and two princesses centre-stage.

Officially, Victory-in-Europe Day was 8 May. In practice, the celebrations lasted at least three days, with attention directed at Buckingham Palace, and with the Royal Family in starring roles throughout.
By mid-afternoon on VE-Day itself, the number of people gathered
in the hot sunshine round the Queen Victoria Memorial in front of
the Palace exceeded that at the Coronation. It was, according to *The
Times*, 'a red, white and blue crowd,' with every other woman wearing
a multi-coloured ribbon or rosette in her hair. Winston Churchill
arrived in an open car and spoke briefly, before disappearing for lunch
with the King and Queen. A lull followed. Then the call 'We want
the King' rose from the crowd. Responding to it, the royal couple
and the two princesses came out onto the balcony, the King in naval,
and Princess Elizabeth in ATS uniform, to be met by prolonged cheering and singing of 'For he's a jolly good fellow'. Only later did the
Prime Minister appear with them, giving the 'V for Victory' sign. In

the evening after Churchill had left, the Royal Family appeared for yet another encore, producing fresh waves of applause and community singing.[1]

That night, they were joined for dinner by a group of Guards officers who were friends of the princesses. After the meal, as the noise continued beyond the railings, Princess Margaret suggested that the younger members of the party should go outside, so that she and her sister could become, for an evening, part of the chorus. It was a frivolous idea which would have been dismissed as absurd on any other day. However, the exhilaration was such that the King and Queen agreed. Accompanied by a police sergeant, a small party left the Palace and went into the street.

They wandered among the chanting, cheering merry-makers. According to Lascelles, 'the Princesses, under escort, went out and walked unrecognized about St. James's Street and Piccadilly'.[2] One member of the group remembers a much more extensive itinerary – from Buckingham Palace to Parliament Square, then to Piccadilly, St. James's Street, Bennet Street, Berkeley Square, Park Lane, and into the Ritz and Dorchester Hotels, before crossing Green Park, and ending up, once again, outside the Palace. 'It was such a happy atmosphere,' he recalls. 'Such a tremendous feeling of being alive.'[3] Apart from Margaret, all were in uniform, making them barely distinguishable from thousands of others also moving almost aimlessly in the no-longer blacked-out city centre.

To be invisible in a crowd! For an instant, the fantasy of being ordinary and unknown became real. After five years of incarceration at Windsor, and a life sentence of the public spotlight, the nation's liberation gave them an exceptional moment of personal freedom. Many years later, Elizabeth recalled that they were terrified of being recognized, 'so I pulled my uniform cap well down over my eyes'. She remembered 'lines of people linking arms and walking down Whitehall, and all of us were swept along by tides of happiness and relief'.[4] One of the party snatched a Dutch sailor's cap as a joke, and the sailor kept chasing after them, not knowing and probably not caring who they had in their midst. In the atmosphere of carefree hysteria, they did the Lambeth Walk and the hokey-cokey. When they got back to the Palace, they stood close to the railings, and helped to orchestrate a new wave of 'We want the King' cries. Unlike most people, however, they were able to supply the King. One of them was sent inside, and shortly afterwards, the King and Queen reappeared on the balcony.[5]

Next day, the holiday continued with street parties and bonfires. During the afternoon, the princesses went with their parents on a tour of bombed-out districts in East London, including a council estate in Stepney, where two blocks of flats, and one hundred and thirty people, had been wiped out by a V2 rocket two months before. The King and Queen and their daughters appeared again on the Palace balcony in the evening, as a military band entertained the crowds from the forecourt.

Similar celebrations followed the Japanese surrender in August, with the important difference that, though the royal participants were the same, a Labour Government was in office, and a Labour Prime Minister now acknowledged the cheers and addressed the crowd. In place of the romantic Churchillian rhetoric, there was a clipped Attleean homily. 'We are right to rejoice at the victory of the people,' declared the new premier, from the balcony of the Ministry of Health, 'and it is right for a short time that we should relax. But I want to remind you that we have a great deal of work to do to win the peace as we won the war.' A speech read by the King, loyally described in the press as 'firm, resonant and strong,' was broadcast through loudspeakers. The Royal Family spent the rest of the day taking curtain calls on the balcony, waving to the multitude, and acknowledging the roars of approval.

That night, the princesses repeated the escapade of 8 May. This time, however, the attempt to behave like anonymous citizens – masked princesses at the ball – did not quite succeed. Perhaps the mood was less euphoric than on VE-Day; perhaps because Princess Elizabeth was not in uniform, she was easier to identify. At any rate, they were spotted. 'Big Crowds at the Palace,' headlined *The Times*. 'Royal Family on the Balcony. Princesses Join the Throng.' The paper revealed that the King's daughters had left the Palace shortly before eleven o'clock, and that they 'were here and there recognised and quickly surrounded by cheering men and women'. But police had told the crowds that 'the princesses wished to be treated as private individuals, and they were allowed to go on their way'.[6]

IN ITSELF, the coming of peace in August did not greatly affect the everyday lives of the Royal Family, who had been re-united at Buckingham Palace earlier in the year. There had already been various symptoms of the post VE-Day phoney peace. Early in August, Elizabeth was taken to Ascot. It was a doubly memorable day. Gordon Richards won five races, carrying the royal colours to victory in the Burghclere Stakes for the first time; and, during lunch at Windsor, the King received the news from President Truman that an atom bomb had been dropped on Hiroshima.[7] Despite such excursions, and weekend trips to Windsor, it took time to re-adjust to the cratered capital and bomb-damaged royal mansion. 'It was a nasty shock to live in a town again,' says Princess Margaret.[8] The King found himself as busy as at the height of the war: the exhortatory use made of the Monarchy, if anything, increased. Peacetime austerity had its own moralising. So did the newly elected Labour Government.

In 1940 the King had favoured Lord Halifax for the premiership. During the war, however, he had grown to like and depend on Churchill, who behaved towards him with extravagant courtesy, and he was distressed by the outcome of the general election in July 1945. Apart from his familiarity with the war leader, and his dislike of change *per se*, he was alarmed about the implications for his family, and his kind. 'Thank God for the Civil Service,' he is supposed to have remarked on hearing of the huge majority for a party committed to a programme of nationalization, redistribution and social reform. In private, he was unapologetically right-wing (his wife even more so), and was often moved to explosions of anger at the latest socialist outrage, especially if he felt he had not been consulted.

He need not have worried. Though he remained much more uneasy about the Attlee governments of 1945 and 1950 than his father had been about the MacDonald ones of 1924 and 1929, there was little in reality that the Labour Cabinet wished or dared to do to discomfort him. Indeed, the new Prime Minister went out of his way to provide reassurance. At Attlee's first audience, George VI expressed disquiet at the news that Hugh Dalton, the renegade son of George V's old tutor Canon Dalton, might be made Foreign Secretary. The Labour premier immediately bowed to the King's wishes, or at least allowed the Palace to think he was doing so. Ernest Bevin became Foreign Secretary, and Dalton was sent to the Treasury instead. Thereafter, Attlee treated the Sovereign with perfect correctness, and there turned out to be as little republicanism in the Labour Party after the Second World War as there had been before it. Soon, what some saw as the incongruity of a King-Emperor presiding over a social revolution – and over the granting of self-rule to the Indian sub-continent, jewel in the imperial crown – became accepted as natural and even valuable. Whereas, in the reign of George V, Buckingham Palace had stood at the pinnacle of a confident Establishment unshaken by the arrival of a Labour Government, in the late 1940s the Royal Family managed to avoid any outward appearance of discomfiture, as the Establishment took some knocks.

Indeed, George VI's passivity arguably became even more of an asset after the war than during it. On the one hand the Royal Family could be seen as a typically British piece of camouflage, disguising and making acceptable the Government's radicalism; on the other, its existence stood as a guarantee that pragmatic caution would prevail, and radicalism kept within bounds. Thus, when Labour took major industries into public ownership (but compensated owners generously) or made adjustments to the powers of the House of Lords (but only modest ones), both left and right thanked God for the Monarchy.

For Elizabeth, peace brought to an end her brief, token excursion into ATS 'normality'. It also produced an increase in the number of her solo engagements. She was nineteen, Honorary Colonel, occasional Counsellor of State, and a performer of royal duties: cast, it was increasingly clear, in the mould of her father and grandfather, though more self-assured than George VI, and cleverer than both of them. Was there ever a moment, in her early adulthood, when she questioned what she did, or wondered, in the prevailing atmosphere of equality, and fashion for the abandoning of pomp and circumstance, whether it was worth it? If she ever indulged in such a dissident speculation, she kept her thoughts to herself. There was no visible hint of rebellion, or suggestion that her own values and those of her parents and mentors ever clashed. She was now the almost certain future Queen, who, if she did succeed, would become the third monarch of the century who had not been born to such a fate but had had it thrust upon them. As the position became clearer with the passage of time, she accepted it, knowing that the possibility of an alternative did not exist.

She did as she was told in an enclosed world where loyal and experienced advice could be taken for granted. She became used to the ritual of the royal speech, consisting of a few platitudes crafted by courtiers skilled at the job. Her itineraries just after the war reflected the priorities of Buckingham Palace, and also of the Government. Thus, in the summer of 1945, she opened a new library of the Royal College of Nursing, presented prizes and certificates to students of the Royal Free Hospital School of Medicine for Women, inspected the Fifth Battalion and Training Battalion of the Grenadier Guards, and addressed (in her recently acquired capacity of Sea Ranger Commodore) three thousand Welsh Girl Guides. She also accompanied her parents on a visit to Ulster, travelling by air for the first time, in a flight from Northolt to Long Kesh.[9]

Some apparently promising requests, however, were refused. Lascelles turned down, on her behalf, an invitation to become the first woman ever to be awarded an honorary degree by Cambridge University – despite pressure from the Chancellor, Lord Baldwin.[10] Occasionally, the proposals of Labour politicians were considered excessive. In 1947, Lascelles rejected a request from Hugh Gaitskell, the Minister of Fuel and Power, for her to attend 'The Miner Comes to Town' exhibition at Marble Arch which had recently been opened by the Prime Minister, on the grounds that she was too busy.[11]

Generally, her visits expressed support for an officially approved, but non-controversial, good cause – though sometimes what the Palace saw as non-controversial turned out to be political dynamite. This was true of a tour of Northern Ireland without her parents in March 1946, for what was described as 'the most ambitious mission undertaken by the young Heir Presumptive'. The tour gave the Princess her first experience of being used, not as a symbol above domestic politics, but as a blatant political tool by one faction.

It was a mission to underline the Union, something which a visit from British royalty, personifying United Kingdom ties, achieved more eloquently than anything. The result was a welcome both vehement

and purposeful. This was a Protestant tour and the groups and institutions she met and addressed reflected it. Sometimes the message
remained implicit. At Dungannon High School 1,200 girls sang 'Come
back to Ulster, dear Princess' to the tune of 'Come back to Erin'. On
other occasions, it was crudely and disagreeably partisan. At Ennis-
killen, the Royal Ulster Constabulary put on a display that included
an illegal still, camouflaged with peat and foliage. The producers of
illicit 'poteen' were acted by local workers, heavily made up with
rouge, and wearing paddy-hats and green three-cornered scarves. An
almost hysterical atmosphere of loyalism lasted until the Princess's
departure from Belfast on 21 March, when a mob of schoolchildren
broke flag-bedecked stands and ran to the edge of the quay. As her
cruiser left the harbour, the whole crowd sang 'Will ye no' come back
again?' and 'Auld Lang Syne'.[12]

In Northern Ireland, enthusiasm was a symptom of sectarian anxiety. Elsewhere and on other occasions, the excitement the Heiress
caused is less easily explicable, especially so soon after the election of
a Government committed to dispossessing the better off. At the beginning of 1946, support for socialism was at its zenith: Gallup put
Labour twenty per cent ahead in the polls, as the Cabinet prepared
to introduce its most radical measures.[13] Yet, such popularity – and
apparent popular support for levelling down – was not accompanied
by any decline in pro-royal sentiment. In April, a gigantic crowd came
to watch the bands of the Royal Horse and Grenadier Guards playing
on the East Terrace of Windsor Castle, to mark Princess Elizabeth's
twentieth birthday. *The Times* estimated it at 40,000, a figure three
times as large as for any such event in the 1930s.[14] Perhaps the austerity
and restrictions, as great after the war as during it, sparked a reaction.
Such gatherings, and the carnival mood that infused them, may have
been a form of escape, a release from drabness. But there was also a
deep personal interest in the Princess: in her beauty, her clothes, her
shy smile, and, increasingly, her prospects.

When and whom would she marry? The assumption was that she
would do so soon; this, after all, had been the point of her education.
'That the Heiress to the Throne would stay unmarried', as Crawfie
archly but accurately put it, 'was unthinkable'.[15] The matter had been
discussed in the popular papers since the 1930s. The difficulty lay in

finding a suitable consort, at a time when suitability still entailed reasons of state. No heir to the throne had ever contracted a marriage for reasons that did not take dynastic considerations into account. However, conventions were changing. Although Edward VIII had been refused permission to marry the woman of his choice, the marriage of George VI had been a non-arranged, romantic and successful one. It was now accepted that a husband could not be forced upon the Princess. It was also accepted, however, that she could not be allowed unrestricted freedom, and that the range of possible suitors was limited to the diaspora of European royalty, few of whom were now in reigning families, and to the upper ranks of the British aristocracy. Though the Princess was well known, she did not know many people. Moreover, her small circle of friends, acquaintances and sufficiently distant relatives included hardly any young men who would be acceptable as a consort, or who would presume to such a role. That she was desirable, there was no question: but to pay court to the Heiress to the world's premier Monarchy required an exceptional degree of passion, confidence or gall.

Perhaps she sensed these difficulties, for in practice they never arose. There were minor flirtations, and stories of heirs to great titles who took liberties and were frozen out for ever. But there was never a phase of boyfriends, of falling in and out of love, of trial and error. From early in her adolescence she took a friendly and romantic interest in one man, and there is no evidence that she ever seriously considered anybody else. 'She fell in love with him,' says one former courtier.[16] According to another, it was a matter of coming contentedly to terms with what had to be. 'There really was no one else she could possibly marry but Prince Philip.'[17] Yet if Philip was, in a sense, hand-picked, it was not the Princess's parents, or the Court, who did the picking.

Prince Philip of Greece, nearly five years older than the Princess, had several commanding advantages: he was royal, on first acquaintance extremely personable and, though not British, he gave an excellent impression of being so. The British Royal Family had known him since he was a small child, when he had taken tea at Buckingham Palace with Queen Mary, who reported him 'a nice little boy with very blue eyes'.[18] He had been in the company of Princess Elizabeth at several pre-war family gatherings, including the wedding of the

Duke and Duchess of Kent in 1934, and the Coronation three years later. Even before the Coronation, Philip's name had been linked in the press with that of the Princess, as one of a tiny list of hypothetical bridegrooms.[19] The first significant encounter, however, took place on 22 July 1939, during the short interlude between the Canada-America trip and the outbreak of war, in the course of a Royal Family visit to the Royal Naval College, Dartmouth. According to Crawfie, the introduction took place in the nursery of the house of the Captain of the College. Philip, who had recently been admitted as a cadet, was taken in to see the princesses, who were playing with a clockwork train. Allegedly, the new friendship was sealed with ginger crackers and lemonade, and by a game of tennis.[20] As far as the adult, non-nursery world was concerned, however, the first important meeting took place at a tea party on board the royal yacht *Victoria and Albert*. This had been arranged – engineered might conceivably be a better word – by Lord Mountbatten, the King's cousin and Philip's uncle. 'Philip came back aboard *V & A* for tea and was a great success with the children,' Mountbatten wrote in his diary.[21] There is also a photographic record of the day. One amateur snap shows the Greek cadet and the much smaller princess together alone, apart from the watching photographer, playing croquet in the Captain's garden. Another picture encapsulates the whole drama, as if it were a tableau: the child-like, solemn Princess Elizabeth, looking much younger than thirteen in a sea of adult faces, her parents and sister, Philip, laughing at some private joke, Mountbatten, also smiling, at his shoulder.

'It is hard to believe,' suggests Mountbatten's official biographer, discussing his subject's attitude towards the 1939 Dartmouth meeting, that 'no thought crossed his mind that an admirable husband for the future Queen Elizabeth might be readily available'.[22] In view of Mountbatten's character, his personal and dynastic ambition, his taste for intrigue, it is more than hard. We may take it for granted. It is possible that such a thought had also occurred to the King and Queen. They were aware, after all, of the need to find a son-in-law before very long, and a foreign prince training for the British Navy was an obvious possibility. In Philip's case, however, there were some worrying features.

Indeed, the Prince's origins and early life raised the question of what 'royal' meant, if it was to be treated as a qualification. Should it be defined in terms of bloodlines, or did it relate to real-world wealth, reputation, and constitutional significance? By the first criterion, Philip was unquestionably royal, in one sense more so than Princess Elizabeth, for he had royalty on both sides of his family, instead of just one. He also happened to be related to the Princess several times over. His most important relationship was through his mother, Princess Alice of Battenberg, who was sister to Lord Mountbatten, mentor and cousin to George VI. But there were also other strands. He was even a fourth cousin once removed through collateral descendants of George III.[23] Moreover, he was not just descended from royalty, he had been born into a reigning Royal Family, the grandson and nephew of Greek kings.

On the other hand, by the second criterion, the current standing of his dynasty, Philip scored badly, or not at all. His birth took place at the Greek royal residence of Mon Repos on the Ionian island of Corfu in June 1921. This did not remain his home for long. Within eighteen months, following the passing of a death sentence by a Greek revolutionary court on his father, Prince Andrew, he and all his family became refugees. A few years later, Philip's mother recorded her thanks to George V for his personal intervention, 'realizing the deadly peril' her husband was in, to ensure that a warship got him 'out of the clutches of the military dictators and brought him and his family away from Greece' on the day after the trial.[24] The exile of Andrew, his wife, four daughters and baby son, turned out effectively to be permanent. Dispossessed, impoverished and in the case of Prince Andrew embittered, they settled in a house provided by Philip's aunt, Marie Bonaparte, at St. Cloud, on the outskirts of Paris.

It was to be a shambolic, meagre existence, built on fading dreams and painful memories. Philip's birthplace in Corfu had been lacking in amenities: in the early 1920s, there was no electricity, gas, running hot water or proper heating.[25] But it had been grand in style, and magnificent in location. By contrast, the villa in St. Cloud was humiliatingly unpretentious, 'a very simple country house,' according to one of Philip's sisters.[26] Cut off from the friendships and rivalries that mattered to him, Prince Andrew, the former commander of armies, immersed himself in the writing of a book appropriately called

Towards Disaster, about the military endeavours, and their failure, for which he had stood trial. His wife, with five children to care for, suffered a nervous breakdown, and turned to religion. The couple separated in 1930, Andrew eventually moving to Monte Carlo, where he died in December 1944.

Against this troubled background, Philip began a cultural shift. Later, there was the question of whether 'Philip the Greek' was ever Greek at all; although born a Greek citizen, the son of a Greek prince, there were no 'ethnic' Greeks in his recent ancestry. In some ways this helped, but it also laid him open to a more damning charge. The description of him as a 'blond Viking', partly on the basis of his Danish ancestry, became a way of avoiding the fact, embarrassing in the 1940s, that his strongest family links were with Germany. All his four sisters married Germans and reverted to a German identity.

Until Philip was adult, he really belonged to no nation, except the freemasonry of Romanov, Habsburg and Saxe-Coburg-Gotha descendants, which conferred an entry ticket to the great houses and palaces of Europe. It was the benign interest of his mother's relatives, and perhaps a family appreciation that England was the most hopeful place for an uprooted royal to seek his fortune, that pushed him in a British direction. From early childhood, there were frequent English trips, especially to see Philip's Battenberg grandmother, the Marchioness of Milford Haven, herself the eldest grandchild of Queen Victoria and sister of the last Tsarina. Sophie ('Tiny'), youngest of Philip's sisters, recalls annual visits by the children to the Marchioness in the 1920s. She remembers sunbathing on the roof at Kensington Palace, where the old lady had an apartment, meetings with members of the British Royal Family, and most influential of all, being regaled with stories of their Europe-wide connections, which contrasted so dramatically with the life they lived in St. Cloud. These expeditions served as a reminder, and a tonic: if the children had any doubt about their social standing, the Marchioness removed them.

At about the time of his parents' separation, Philip left the American school in St. Cloud at which he had been a pupil, and was sent to Cheam, an English preparatory establishment in Surrey; and from there to Salem, in Baden, a school owned by one of his German brothers-in-law and run by the legendary Kurt Hahn. But for Hitler, the rest of his education might have been German. In 1934, however, Hahn moved to Scotland to escape the Nazis, setting up a new school, Gordonstoun. Philip became a pupil and, as a result, in the words of the Countess of Airlie, was 'brought up to all intents and purposes an Englishman,'[27] except that few Englishmen ever had to suffer the rigours and eccentricities of the Hahn–Gordonstoun form of educational progressiveness.

'I don't think anybody thinks I had a father,' Philip allegedly once complained. 'Most people think that Dickie's my father anyway.'[28] Philip had been much affected by the breakdown of his parents' marriage, and retained a great sympathy for Prince Andrew. 'He really loved his father,' says one close associate. 'He had a big image of him which persisted, and his death was a great shock to him.'[29] After 1930, however, he saw much more of his mother, Princess Alice, and was closer to her, despite all her difficulties – which were extreme. In addition to the psychological problems which developed during Philip's childhood, she was congenitally deaf. Later, she used to say that she could not communicate with her children until they were old enough to speak, when she became able to read their lips.[30] But the presentation of her as a demented recluse was false. Friends recall her, except when ill, as forceful, intelligent and amusing. Despite her marital and other difficulties, she was responsible for translating her husband's book from Greek into English. Conceivably, as one friend of Philip puts it, her eventual decision to found a Greek Orthodox monastic order, and become a nun in it, 'was a very clever solution to the problem of how she fitted into the world,' as an elderly royal widow without money, but with an interest in good causes.[31]

Nevertheless, Philip's early life, with an absent father and often psychologically absent mother, was by any standards disturbed and unstable. Much of it, especially when his mother had to go into a sanatorium, was spent migrating between schools and foster-homes provided by relatives. There was a confusion: uncertainty, neglect, and the feeling of being special mixed together. The only son, as well as the youngest child, Philip was a particular focus of family attention, especially to his four sisters who adored, petted and mothered him. However, within the space of a few months in 1931–2 all of them solved the problem of a disintegrating home by marrying German princes, scattering what was left of his family across Europe.

There were fixed points: Salem, for summer holidays, was one. When Philip was at school in Britain, his Uncle George, Marquess of Milford Haven and son of the dowager Marchioness, provided another, becoming his guardian in school vacations, and helping with fees. Although George was his main benefactor, Philip was also a frequent visitor at the house of his other uncle, Lord Mountbatten. 'He was around with us a lot from about 1934,' says Patricia.[32] Another refuge was Gordonstoun where Philip became a model pupil – athletic, outgoing, enterprising, effortlessly displaying precisely those attributes which it had been Hahn's vision to produce.

Yet the standard portrayal of Philip in his teens as a kind of *Boys' Own Paper* hero misses something out. There was a picaresque quality, the sense of the adventurer who lives by his wits, and for whom what one early writer called 'the lean upbringing of expatriate royalty,'[33] had provided as keen a training as any continental theory. Philip's cousin Alexandra, Queen of Yugoslavia (and a fellow expatriate), recalled him on holiday with her family in Venice, a year before the Dartmouth meeting, as a genial sponger, living in a style not uncommon among displaced princelings, and giving the impression of 'a huge hungry dog, perhaps a friendly collie who had never had a basket of his own'.[34]

The summer of 1938 was an especially waif-like moment. George Milford Haven had died the previous April, leaving Prince Philip, as Philip Ziegler puts it, 'stateless, nameless and not far from penniless'[35] and particularly in need of open-handed friends. Luckily, more substantial help was available. The death of one benefactor cleared the way for another, of incomparably greater influence. Observing Philip's predicament, George's younger brother Louis – 'Uncle Dickie' – stepped in, and took over what remained of the job of bringing his nephew up. It was a generous undertaking, but also, in view of the young man's obvious talents, a well judged one. Lord Mountbatten was a prominent naval officer and it had, in any case, already been planned that the best place for a *déraciné* young prince with a taste for travel, and no home base, was the British Navy. Hence, on 1 May 1939, Philip joined Dartmouth College as a Special Entry Cadet.

When Prince Philip and Princess Elizabeth met in July, he was an unknown young man barely two months into training. What did he make of his world-famous distant cousin, with her home in Buckingham Palace? Did he distinguish between the celebrity and the child-like person? It would be surprising if she did not have an impact, because of who she was: but it would also be surprising if, at this stage, Philip's interest was romantic. Handsome and confident eighteen-year-old young men are not often greatly attracted by thirteen-year-old little girls scarcely out of short socks. According to Queen Alexandra, the previous summer the Greek prince had shown himself a girl-crazy party-goer on the Venetian social scene. 'Blondes, brunettes and red head charmers,' she recalled, 'Philip gallantly and I think quite impartially squired them all.'[36] Hélène Cordet, a cabaret singer who had been a childhood friend (and who was later dubbed by the French press as 'the mystery blonde' and 'the one who will *not* be invited to the wedding') had a similar view of him.[37] Other accounts also show him as a happy-go-lucky enjoyer of female company, and player of the field. Yet Princess Elizabeth was pretty, royal, and obviously a catch. The thoughts that must have passed through his uncle's mind, may also have passed through his own. At the time, however, there were other pressing things to consider. War was imminent, with everything that such a prospect offered to a prize-winning naval cadet, with excellent connections.

If the British Royal Family had a good war, Philip in a more conventional sense, had a highly distinguished one. After a period of escorting contingents of troops from Australia to the Middle East, he was involved in several engagements in the Mediterranean. During the battle of Matapan against the Italian fleet, he controlled the searchlights of his ship, and was mentioned in dispatches. 'Thanks to his alertness and appreciation of the situation,' reported his Captain, 'we were able to sink in five minutes two eight-inch-gun Italian cruisers.'[38] Philip spent much of 1941 with the British Fleet in the East Mediterranean. In the spring, Greek resistance to the Germans crumbled, and on 23 April, King George of Greece and his Government were evacuated to Crete. The same day, Princess Elizabeth wrote to Winston Churchill thanking him for a bunch of roses he and his wife had sent her for her fifteenth birthday two days earlier. In her letter, she offered her sympathy, in view of the 'very worrying time' he had lately been having.[39] Perhaps she had Philip's recent dangers and exploits, and those of his royal house, partly in mind.

Such an officer was likely to be rapidly promoted in wartime, especially if he had ambition. In Philip's case, the energy and drive he had shown at Gordonstoun and Dartmouth, together with a view of his own long-term future which received ample encouragement from his Uncle Dickie, helped to push him forward. Mike Parker, a fellow officer who had also been a fellow cadet and later became his equerry, recalls thinking of the Prince as a dedicated professional and as a man heading for the very top: somebody who already 'had mapped out a course to which he was going to stick . . . a plan already in his mind that had probably been set before he left'.[40] In October 1942, Philip was made First Lieutenant and second-in-command of a destroyer, at twenty-one one of the youngest officers to hold such a post.

His adventures continued. The following July, while courtiers in Buckingham Palace exchanged learned memoranda about the date of Princess Elizabeth's coming-of-age and its constitutional significance, Prince Philip was aboard HMS *Wallace* off the coast of Sicily, helping to provide cover for the Allied attack and possibly bombarding one of his brothers-in-law, on the German side, in the process. In July 1944, his ship was sent to the Pacific, where he remained until after the dropping of atomic bombs on Hiroshima and Nagasaki, and until the final surrender of Japan.[41]

> Wherein I spake of most disastrous chances,
> Of moving accidents by flood and field,
> Of hair-breadth 'scapes, i' the imminent deadly breach . . .
> My story being done,
> She gave me for my pains a world of sighs.

It is hard to think of an experience of war further removed than that of the Heiress Presumptive, in her castellated schoolroom.

At first, Philip's busy war provided little scope for contact with the British Royal Family. Shore leaves were brief, makeshift and hectic. Parker felt that it was a bond between him and Prince Philip that both of them were 'orphans' (Parker was Australian), with a problem about where to stay.[42] In London, Philip was often put up by the Mountbattens, who had been bombed out of previous homes and were living in a house in Chester Street. Mountbatten's younger daughter Pamela recalls that she and a camp bed would move from room to room to provide space for her cousin, who would 'come and go and added glamour and sparkle to every occasion'.[43] His favours were distributed widely. Queen Alexandra, herself in London at the time, maintained that 'the fascination of Philip had spread like influenza, I knew, through a whole string of girls'.[44] But there was no special girlfriend. According to Parker, 'never once did I ever find him involved with any particular one. It was very much in a crowd formation'.[45] Other stories about Philip in wartime confirm the impression of a hedonistic, though also cashless, socialite whose uniform, looks, charm and connections opened every door – a character out of Evelyn Waugh or Olivia Manning, who popped up wherever in the world there were enough members of the pre-war upper class to hold a party.

Princess Elizabeth was sometimes in his thoughts. Alexandra met up with him in 1941 in Cape Town, where he was on leave from a troop ship. When she came across him writing a letter, he told her it was to 'Lilibet'. Alexandra assumed – such were the mental processes of displaced royalty – that he was fishing for invitations.[46] Perhaps she was right. It was not, however, until the end of 1943 that he was able to accept one of importance. This was to spend Christmas with the Royal Family at Windsor Castle, and to attend the annual Windsor family pantomime.[47] Philip accepted, with pleasure.

It was a private invitation. However, both the show, and the Prince's attendance at it, were reported in the press. In November, it was announced that a stage had been erected in a large hall in the 'country mansion' where the princesses were staying; that a cast of forty was rehearsing under the joint direction of Princess Elizabeth and a local schoolmaster, who had together written the script; and that twenty-five village school children would provide the chorus, accompanied by a Guards band.[48] A few days before Christmas, *The Times* reported that 'Prince Philip of Greece' had attended the third of three performances, sitting in the front row. Others in the audience included the King and Queen, various courtiers, royal relatives, and villagers.[49]

According to Lisa Sheridan, Prince Philip was more than just a passive spectator of the seventeen-year-old Elizabeth as she acted, joked, tap-danced and sang a few songs just in front of him. 'Both in the audience and in the wings he thoroughly entered into the fun, and was welcomed by the princesses as a delightful boy cousin.'[50] The pantomime was followed by Christmas festivities. On Boxing Day, there was a family meal at the Castle including retainers, Prince Philip and the young Marquess of Milford Haven. 'After dinner, and some charades,' Sir Alan Lascelles recorded in his diary, 'they rolled back the carpet in the crimson drawing-room, turned on the gramophone, and frisked and capered away till near 1 a.m.'[51]

Crawfie maintained it was a turning point: thereafter, Elizabeth took a growing interest in Philip's activities and whereabouts, and exchanged letters with him. The Heiress to the throne enjoyed the idea of being like other girls, she suggested, with a young man in the services to write to.[52]

IF ELIZABETH only began to think seriously about Philip in December 1943, she was way behind the drifting circuit of European royalty and its hangers on, which had been talking about the supposed relationship, almost as if a marriage was a *fait accompli*, for two or three years. Of course, Philip's eligibility as a bachelor prince, together with his semi-Britishness, was likely to make him the subject of conjecture in any case. However, before the end of 1943, the couple had little opportunity to get to know each other. What is curious, therefore, is the firmness of the predictions, and the confidence of the rumours, from quite early in the war.

One of the first to pick up and record the story of an intended marriage, in its definite form, was Chips Channon, befriender of Balkan princelings. He heard it at the beginning of 1941 during a visit to Athens, where the tale seemed to be current among the Greek Royal Family, whose interest had been sharpened by the presence of Prince Philip in their midst, on leave from his ship. After meeting Philip at a cocktail party, Channon noted in his diary, 'He is to be our Prince Consort, and that is why he is serving in our Navy.' The alliance between the British and Greek royal houses had supposedly been arranged by the finessing hand of Philip's uncle, Lord Mountbatten. Philip was handsome and charming, noted Channon, 'but I deplore such a marriage. He and Princess Elizabeth are too inter-related.'[53]

Such an item was, of course, no more than gossip, a symptom of the decadence and anxieties of the Greek court. Princess Elizabeth was fourteen at the time, and the notion of the British Government or Royal Family fixing a future marriage alliance with the Greek one is preposterous. According to Mountbatten a few years later, it was at about this time that Philip 'made up his mind and asked me to apply for [British] naturalisation for him'.[54] Perhaps it was news of this plan, combined with Philip's evident closeness to his British uncle, that inspired the tale. Nevertheless, the existence of such a lively and, as it turned out accurate, rumour nearly three years before a serious friendship is supposed to have started, puts the Prince's visit to witness the Princess performing into perspective. Had Mountbatten been involved behind the scenes? It is possible. 'He was a shrewd operator and intriguer, always going round corners, never straight at it,' says one former courtier from the 1940s, 'he was ruthless in his approach to the royals.'[55] Another suggests: 'Dickie seems to have planned it in his own mind, but it was not an arranged marriage.'[56] It would certainly have been in character for him to have followed up on the 1939 introduction. That, however, is a matter for speculation. What is clear is that in the course of 1944, despite the huge pressures on him, Lord Mountbatten took it upon himself to follow through his match-making initiative with operational resolve.

One effect of the Christmas 1943 get-together, and of its publication in the press, was to fuel the rumours. Prince Philip himself was reticent. Parker knew that Philip had begun to visit the Royal Family when he was in England, but he did not find out the significance of the visits until after the war.[57] Others had more sensitive antennae. In February 1944, Channon again got the story, this time from a source very close to the throne – his own parents-in-law, Lord and Lady Iveagh, who had just taken tea with the King and Queen. The Windsor party had evidently been a success. 'I do believe,' Channon reaffirmed, 'that a marriage may well be arranged one day between Princess Elizabeth and Prince Philip of Greece.'[58] Meanwhile, in Egypt, where the Greek royal family presided over the Government-in-exile, interest had deepened, and with good reason. Within months, or possibly a few weeks, of the Windsor meeting, Philip had declared his intentions to the Greek king. The diary of Sir Alan Lascelles contains a significant entry for 2 April 1944 in which he records that George VI had told him that Prince Philip of Greece had recently asked his uncle, George of Greece, whether he thought he could be considered as a suitor for the hand of Princess Elizabeth. The proposition had been rejected.[59] However, it was early days.

In August 1944, the British ambassador, Sir Miles Lampson, recorded meeting Prince Philip, once again on leave, at a ball in Alexandria, in the company of the Greek crown prince and princess. Lampson found him 'a most attractive youth'. In the course of the evening, the crown princess let slip 'that Philip would do very well for Princess Elizabeth!' an idea now of long-standing, and one on which the beleaguered Greek royal family was evidently pinning high hopes.

Philip's presence in Egypt, however, inspired more than a minor indiscretion from a relative. On 23 August, according to Lampson, Lord Mountbatten, now Supreme Allied Commander in South East Asia, arrived in Cairo by air and proceeded to unfold a most extraordinary cloak-and-dagger tale. The purpose of his mission, Mountbatten explained as they drove to the embassy from the aerodrome, was to arrange for Prince Philip, 'being a very promising officer in the British Navy,' to apply for British nationality. Gravely, Mountbatten explained that King George VI had become concerned about the depleted numbers of his close relatives, and believed that, if Philip became properly British, 'he should be an additional asset to the British Royal Family and a great help to them in carrying out their royal functions'. It was therefore his intention, he continued, to sound out Philip, and then the king of Greece, about his proposition. In the course of the same day, both were sounded, together with the crown prince, and all three agreed. Early that afternoon, a satisfied Mountbatten left by aeroplane for Karachi to resume his Command.[60]

What should we make of this very curious account? Mountbatten's explanation for his 'soundings' is obviously unconvincing – the one thing the British Monarchy did not need was functional help from a young foreign royal, let alone a Greek one, just because he happened